# The Fabian Society

The Fabian Society is Britain's leading left of centre think tank and political society, committed to creating the political ideas and policy debates which can shape the future of progressive politics.

With over 300 Fabian MPs, MEPs, Peers, MSPs and AMs, the Society plays an unparalleled role in linking the ability to influence policy debates at the highest level with vigorous grassroots debate among our growing membership of over 7000 people, 70 local branches meeting regularly throughout Britain and a vibrant Young Fabian section organising its own activities. Fabian publications, events and ideas therefore reach and influence a wider audience than those of any comparable think tank. The Society is unique among think tanks in being a thriving, democratically-constituted membership organisation, affiliated to the Labour Party but organisationally and editorially independent.

For over 120 years Fabians have been central to every important renewal and revision of left of centre thinking. The Fabian commitment to open and participatory debate is as important today as ever before as we explore the ideas, politics and policies which will define the next generation of progressive politics in Britain, Europe and around the world. Find out more at **www.fabian-society.org.uk**

Fabian Society
11 Dartmouth Street
London SW1H 9BN
www.fabian-society.org.uk

Fabian ideas
Series editor: Jonathan Heawood

First published 2005

ISBN 0 7163 0617 4
ISSN 1746-1146

British Library Cataloguing in Publication data.
A catalogue record for this book is available from the British Library.


Printed by Bell & Bain, Glasgow

# The Politics of Pension Reform

by

Richard Brooks and
John Denham MP

# About the authors

**Richard Brooks** is the Fabian Society's Research Director. Richard joined the Fabian Society in 2004 from the Institute for Public Policy Research, where he co-authored *A New Contract for Retirement* in 2002. He is also the lead councillor responsible for resources, including pensions, in the London Borough of Tower Hamlets.

**John Denham** is MP for Southampton Itchen, which he has represented since the 1992 general election. He was Minister of State for Pensions in 1998-99 during the publication of the government's 1998 Green Paper *Partnership in Pensions*, and has held a number of other ministerial positions. He is currently the chair of the Home Affairs Select Committee.

**Digby Jones** became Director General of the CBI in 2000, initially for a five year period that has subsequently been extended to seven years. He was previously a vice chairman of KPMG and prior to that senior partner of Edge and Ellison, working in the field of corporate finance. He fulfils a wide variety of non-executive roles including many at voluntary and charitable organisations.

**C BII**
THE VOICE OF BUSINESS
40 YEARS

**Brendan Barber** has been the General Secretary of the Trades Union Congress since 2003, prior to which he was deputy General Secretary to John Monks. He has worked at the TUC for thirty years in a variety of roles addressing the full spectrum of labour issues. He is also a non-executive director of the Court of the Bank of England.

*TUC*

**Ian Naismith** is an actuary who is currently Head of Pensions and Market Development at Scottish Widows. As well as editing Scottish Widows' technical magazine for financial advisers, *techtalk*, he writes extensively for the trade press, is a regular speaker at industry conferences, represents the company's viewpoint to government and industry bodies, and is involved in

SCOTTISH WIDOWS

product development. He is a member of the ABI's Pensions Committee and chairman of the Pensions (Tax) Panel.

**Alison O'Connell** was appointed as the first Director of the Pensions Policy Institute in 2002. As an actuary she was involved in pricing life and health insurance products, then spent 10 years as a strategy consultant in the financial services industry, first at McKinsey &
Co., then independently. She later became Head of Strategy for the Swiss Reinsurance Group. She became a Fellow of the Institute of Actuaries in 1988. Her interest in pension policy grew out of questioning the 'demographic time bomb' and 'state versus private' arguments of the 1990s.

**Chris Curry** joined the PPI as Research Director in July 2002 from the Association of British Insurers where he had been Senior Economist. His pension background led to work there on the analysis of stakeholder pensions, the Pension Credit and annuities. Prior to this, Chris was an Economic Adviser at the Department of Social Security, where his work included analytical support for the Pension Provision Group, and working on the subsequent Pensions Green Paper published in December 1998.

**Christine Farnish** took up post as Chief Executive of the National Association of Pension Funds in 2002. The Association is the leading voice of workplace pension provision in the UK, and Christine leads the
NAPF's policy and representational work. Christine joined the NAPF from the Financial Services Authority, where she was Consumer Director from 1998 to 2002. Prior to that she worked for OFTEL and in local government.

The authors would like to thank Scottish Widows for their support and assistance in bringing this project to fruition.

# Contents

# Part One
# The Politics of Pension Reform

Richard Brooks and
John Denham MP

'On pensions, our aim is a system that provides security and decency for all, which encourages and rewards saving, and is financially sustainable. And because, more than anything, people need certainty to plan for the future we will seek a national consensus—cross-party, cross-generation—for long-term reform.'

'We need to forge a national consensus about how we move from a pension system designed for today's pension problems to one that is right for tomorrow's. We appointed the Pensions Commission to look into the future of pensions and its second report is due in autumn 2005.We are clear about the goals of a reformed system. It must tackle poverty, provide everyone with the opportunity to build an adequate retirement income, and be affordable, fair and simple to understand. In particular it must address the disadvantages faced by women.'

Labour Party Manifesto 2005

# Introduction

The politics of pension reform is just as important as the policy itself. This autumn, Adair Turner's Pensions Commission will provide its analysis of the options in what will be a critical moment for the debate. But even the best technical analysis will not guarantee that the right choices will be made. Only if we get the politics right as well as the detail of the reform package can the government achieve what has eluded its predecessors and achieve a pensions settlement which endures for future generations.

Consensus needs to be built among the expert stakeholders—and most importantly among the public—around some key issues. But what do we mean by 'consensus?' There will never be a perfect consensus about the right pensions system for the UK, and consensus does not mean everyone agreeing about everything. What is crucial is that there is enough consensus to make reform politically possible in the short term and politically durable in the long term. We are some way from that point at the moment.

Government has a key role in developing such a consensus. The first step is for ministers to be clear in their own minds about how much agreement they require and on which issues. The government then has a unique role in building consensus by bringing together the major stakeholders—employers, employees, pension providers, pensioners and other representative groups—and focusing them on the key issues. Individual organisations promoting their own ideas in competition with each other give us a healthy debate. However, government needs to bring these organisations together so that they can try to make the necessary trade-offs that will bring this process to a resolution. The stakeholder organisations, for their part, need to commit to the process of achieving consensus through the prioritisation of their objectives and ultimately compromise.

But consensus among the expert stakeholders is not enough to create a durable pensions settlement. That requires broad and deep public consent of the kind that sustains institutions such as the NHS. The pensions system must meet a set of 'technical' objectives including the prevention of poverty, the provision of incentives to save, and afford-ability to the public purse in both the short and long term. But it must also meet a set of subjective tests by which the public is likely to judge it, including: 'Does it work for me?' 'What do I get out for what I put in?' 'Is it fair to me and to others?' 'Does it reward responsibility and discourage irresponsibility?' 'Do I understand it?' These tests are just as important as any others.

Our assessment of the current debate leads us to make two central recommendations to government about how it should prioritise the issues. Firstly, it should build on the existing consensus that the Basic State Pension is inadequate. Secondly, for this to be an effective founda-tion of a comprehensive package government must get stakeholders to focus on two issues where they have considerable disagreements: what sort of further support the state should make for second pensions; and how the overall package should be financed. We see these as the two most important and most contentious issues to be resolved at this stage. But focusing on these issues depends on keeping the controversial but secondary debate about compulsion in context.

One of our central conclusions is that a revitalised first tier state pension, currently provided by the Basic State Pension, should be at the heart of a new pensions strategy. This would be set at the poverty-prevention level of the Guarantee Credit, currently £109.45 per week for a single pensioner, and would be indexed to earnings and not prices.

Such a reform would dramatically cut pensioner poverty, improve incentives to save and radically simplify the system. It is supported by a wide range of stakeholder groups and even more importantly is in tune with public expectations. Nonetheless it is hugely ambitious.

This kind of reform would be very expensive. There are a range of options for how to pay for it, including tax or National Insurance rises, diverting other public spending, and diverting other state pensions spending. However, there is little consensus about the appropriate funding mechanism. The first key building block of consensus is thus to confirm the level of support for an enhanced first tier state pension, and seek views about how to pay for it. Consensus around first tier reform would be a solid foundation for wider agreement.

The other key issue concerns what sort of second pension and other support for pension saving the state should provide in addition to an adequate first tier. In the current pensions debate, a number of commentators argue that if the state could guarantee an adequate basic state pension, it could withdraw from any responsibility (other than prudential regulation) for second pension provision. Others argue that, for most people, even a much more generous basic pension is so far below their aspirations for retirement that the state will have to maintain some interest in their second pensions.

There are strong arguments on either side. If the state only provides a first-tier pension, it could divert all other pension resources into its funding. This could include the resources that are currently earmarked for National Insurance rebates and, in the future, monies that would have to be paid out through the State Second Pension. It could also include the very significant sums of money foregone on tax relief for pension contributions.

On the other hand, even with an enhanced basic pension many people might expect the state to continue to assist in the provision or at least the funding of their second pension. There is a particularly strong case for helping people who may find it difficult to make pension savings because they are on modest incomes or have periods of caring, but for whom a pension of £109.45 per week would represent a poor proportion of their typical earnings. Many of these people are women and as the Government has recognised there is an increasingly vocal lobby that wants to tackle past and current discrimination against women in the pension system. It would be politically very difficult to withdraw the State Second Pension which has been introduced precisely to assist this group and those whose working lives are interrupted by caring responsibilities without making some equally generous provision.

Any state support for second pensions should meet some key tests. Building on the basic pension it should enable most people to retire on a reasonable proportion of their working income. It should clearly incentivise personal responsibility and saving. It should target more support on those people with low incomes who find it difficult to make additional savings, including carers and others with intermittent working lives. Most importantly of course, it should be seen to be fair. The current system of tax relief achieves none of these objectives and should be overhauled.

Pensions policy is bedevilled by fashion, and the issue around which the debate is currently focused is that of compulsion. Yet compulsion may be a means but can never be an end in itself. Compulsion is also a confused issue with many aspects—compulsion could apply to employers or individuals to join, provide or contribute to a pension scheme. There is a good degree of consensus that individuals should be required to opt out of their employer pension scheme rather than opt in as at present.

But there is little consensus about the desirability of additional compulsion on either employers or individuals to contribute to a second pension. With the important exception of bringing the self-employed properly into the National Insurance system, we believe that additional compulsion on individuals would be undesirable in the absence of a reform to the first tier which addressed the current incentive problems. However, we do not think that additional compulsion to save should be ruled out indefinitely. The time scale of the problems it is meant to address means there should not be an artificial sense of urgency over this issue.

At the moment there is not sufficiently broad consensus to allow the government to undertake the necessary radical reform of our pensions system. Neither is there sufficiently deep consensus to make a set of reforms durable over the long term. Nonetheless, we believe that such a consensus can be built, and once this has been done it would be possible to introduce some independent oversight of the reformed system. Government needs to focus the debate on the critical issues, and the stakeholders need to commit to the process in a meaningful way. All parties need to remember that the ultimate arbiters of pensions policy are the public. In the long term, theirs is the only consensus that matters.

# 1 | Political and Policy Context

The pensions debate in the UK is at a critical point. Labour's general election manifesto made it clear that the party intends to undertake a serious reform of the UK pensions system in its third term. It also explicitly recognised the need to seek consensus if such reform is to be durable. For anyone concerned with pension provision in the UK this should be a very welcome starting point.

The government has indicated its willingness to engage in a national debate on reform of the pensions system. The new Secretary of State, David Blunkett, has said that he wants to build consensus about the way forward. The Pensions Commission will report in autumn 2005 with its analysis of policy options to improve pension provision.

It is important to recognise that there is no short-term pensions crisis in the UK. Although there have been serious problems with a number of occupational pension schemes, and a significant group of pensioners still live in poverty, a crisis is by definition unstable and unsustainable, and those are not the characteristics of our present situation. Instead there are a number of serious and interrelated longer term problems with the pensions environment in the UK. These include the level of overall pension provision and future pensioner incomes; current and future pensioner poverty; complexity in the pensions environment; and poor incentives for low to middle income savers.

The UK has an ageing population. Not only are people living longer, but the large cohorts of 50s and 60s 'baby boomers' will start retiring in bulk from the end of this decade. Meanwhile UK fertility rates remain below the replacement level, where they have been since the 1970s. The combined effect of these trends will be a sustained increase in the proportion of older people in the population over the next 30 years. It is a simple arithmetical truth that if average pensioner incomes are to maintain their current position relative to the rest of the population, then pensioners' share of national income must rise in line with their share of the population. However, incomes are already too low for many pensioners, with half a million pensioner households living in poverty and average pensioner incomes distorted by the fact that the richest fifth of pensioners do much better than the rest. If we want pensioner living standards to improve relative to the rest of the population then the share of national wealth going to pensions will need to rise even faster than their share of the population.

In the last eight years the government has made a number of major changes to the pensions environment in the UK, including the introduction of the Minimum Income Guarantee and its replacement with the Pension Credit; the replacement of the State Earnings-Related Pension Scheme with the State Second Pension; the introduction of the Pension Protection Fund; and a range of regulatory reforms to private and occupational pensions.

This programme has been motivated by a concern to focus public resources on the poorest pensioners, and it has achieved real improvements for many people. However, it has further increased the complexity of the pension system and has increased pensioner incomes at the costs of extending means testing to much larger numbers of pensioners. It has proved difficult to reduce the proportion of poor pensioners who are entitled to benefits that they are not claiming. Individuals are not clear about what the state will provide for them and what they need to do for themselves, and confidence in both state and private pension systems is low.

Defined benefit pension schemes, which for many employees represent the most desirable form of private provision, have been in decline since the beginning of the 1980s. However, the second half of the 1990s saw the rate of scheme closures increase dramatically and the evidence since 2000 suggests a further acceleration of this trend. Stakeholder pensions, introduced in 2001 as a simple and relatively low-cost personal pension, are a welcome addition to the pensions landscape. However, most stakeholder schemes run by employers are 'empty shells' with no contributions being made. Overall savings rates do not appear to have gone up as a result of their introduction.

This short pamphlet is not the place for a detailed evaluation of the government's track record. The government's stance now reflects a welcome recognition that policy is not adequate to the present challenges for pension provision. Our focus here is on the future—what are the key issues in the next stage of reform, where do the major stakeholder groups stand in relation to them, and how can the necessary consensus be achieved to make reform both politically possible and sufficiently durable?

The right way to think about all of these problems is to start from where we want to be in 40 years time and work backwards, not from today's immediate problems. The government has rightly resisted the kind of short term, populist fixes offered by the Conservative and Liberal Democrat parties, despite the temptation to do so ahead of a general election. Both of these opposition parties wanted to fund an increase in the Basic State Pension by one off reductions in government spending. We should reject this type of unsustainable approach in principle. But the government must be equally cautious about relying on reform to other aspects of the welfare system—such as Incapacity Benefit—to fund pensions. Nor should we assume permanent success in increasing already very high labour market participation rates. Whilst both objectives are good in themselves, any pension system must be resilient over a 50 year horizon in which periods of recession and higher unemployment seem almost inevitable.

Another important context for this pamphlet is provided by Adair Turner's independent Pensions Commission. The Commission's first report, *Pensions: Challenges and Choices* (Pensions Commission, 2004) added to the technical understanding of the challenges facing UK pensions provision and also achieved a number of important political outcomes. It has generated significant pressure on government to proceed with further pension reform, and is due to make its second and final report including policy options in Autumn 2005. Even before the Commission made its first report there was such pressure from independent think-tanks, academics and representative groups. However, the Commission was itself established by government, and it would be highly damaging if government were now seen to ignore the analysis of its own creation.

Of course, we have been here before. The Labour administration set up the the Pension Provision Group headed by Tom Ross in 1997. It made powerful reports in 1999 and 2001. In many ways, its messages were similar to those in the first report from the Turner Commission. What was lacking at that time was the political will to tackle the deepest problems in the system. The Government has raised the stakes further with the Turner Commission and this time must respond.

The Pensions Commission has improved public understanding of the difficult choices facing the UK with regard to pension provision. Its central conclusion concerns the overall level of pension provision and the future incomes of pensioners:

Faced with the increasing proportion of the population aged over 65, society and individuals must choose between four options. Either:

(i) pensioners will become poorer relative to the rest of society; or
(ii) taxes/National Insurance contributions devoted to pensions must rise; or
(iii) savings must rise; or
(iv) average retirement ages must rise.

But the first option (poorer pensioners) appears unattractive; and there are significant barriers to solving the problem through any one of the other three options alone. Some mix of higher taxes/National Insurance contributions, higher savings and later average retirement is required.

Pensions Commission, 2004, Ch.1

The key political point is that *all* of these options appear unattractive, not just the first. One of the most important functions of the Commission's first report has been to increase public awareness that there is no easy answer to the problem of aggregate under-saving. Option one—the 'do nothing' option—leads to relatively poorer pensioners. Options two and three—higher taxes, higher National Insurance contributions or higher private savings—reduce the amount of income that is otherwise available for current consumption by savers. Option four pushes back the retirement age—a particularly sensitive issue for manual workers—and in any case is unlikely to be capable of fully addressing the problem on its own.

So a key political problem is that if pension reform is to be successful and durable then broad public consent must be developed for some combination of relatively unpalatable alternatives. The problems of the UK pensions environment can be addressed, but not without making significant trade-offs. Gaining public consent for these trade-offs is perhaps the most challenging aspect of pension reform in the new Parliament, and a task that requires commitment not just from government but from a wide range of expert and representative bodies also.

However pension provision is organised there are costs and risks to be shared between the many individuals that make up society as a whole. Those who are currently retired have different characteristics and interests from those who are currently working. The distribution of burdens, benefits and incentives across low, middle and higher income savers is another likely area of contention. Employers, employees and the self employed share some concerns and have different interests in other areas. Financial services firms have a key role in achieving public policy objectives as well as owing responsibilities to their shareholders—most of which are probably pension fund managers themselves.

Deciding how to balance these interests is an inherently political activity for which there can be no technical solution. Whether there are technical solutions to informing this decision, achieving consensus and maintaining the chosen balance is another issue that we will return to later. Getting the technical analysis right is extremely important, especially in so far as it can establish an understanding of the problems and the implications of the options that is shared widely amongst the many interested stakeholder groups. However, even with the best technical analysis, if the politics are wrong then the process will fail to produce a sustainable solution. It would be difficult for the Commission to comment directly on these issues and to retain its position of independence. This pamphlet thus attempts to fill that gap and addresses the politics of pensions reform.

The next section discusses the process of achieving the necessary consensus for durable reform. The third section considers some of the key issues, the likely reform options and the political debate in relation to each. The publication closes with a series of responses from key stakeholders: the CBI, the TUC, Scottish Widows and The Pensions Policy Institute.

# 2 | Achieving Consensus

The government has been clear that there needs to be a broad consensus in relation to reform of the pensions system. Both the 2005 manifesto, and the DWP document 'Principles for reform—the national pensions debate' are explicit about this. Indeed, the DWP document sets out a process for achieving such a consensus: first by reaching agreement on the principles that inform our choices, then by achieving a shared factual analysis of the issues (via the work of the Pensions Commission), and finally by moving on to consideration of specific options for reform.

However, this is highly unlikely to be a straightforward, linear process. The government's six principles are that a reformed pension system 'must tackle poverty, provide everyone with the opportunity to build an adequate retirement income, and be affordable, fair and simple to understand. In particular it must address the disadvantages faced by women.' It is very hard to object to these as they stand.

The problem is that there is enormous scope for interpreting these principles in different ways, for giving each of them more or less priority, and for taking into consideration other factors that are of legitimate public concern. To give the principles sufficient content it is necessary to consider them in relation to some specific policy proposals. Consensus building will require proposals to be evaluated in the light of principles, but at the same time it is only specific proposals that make clear the interpretation of the general principles themselves. This pamphlet thus proposes two key, concrete issues around which consensus can and should be built—the basic pension provided by the state, and state support for second pension saving.

Do we need consensus at all? Some commentators argue that in such a complex area, where consensus may be difficult to achieve, what is needed instead is a strong lead from government. Yet despite the difficulties, a degree of consensus is necessary for two reasons. Firstly, consensus is required if reform is to be politically possible in the short term. It is clear that any pension reform which adequately addresses the problems of the current system is likely to require significant sacrifices of current consumption or leisure at the aggregate level. In addition, the distribution of benefits and burdens is likely to change with any significant reform, and the losers are certain to be a more vocal constituency than the winners, who sometimes don't even notice their gains. The potential for all of this to damage the government of the day is obvious, and the potential becomes a near certainty if the atmosphere in which these changes take place is acrimonious.

Secondly, pensions policy should be politically durable in the long term. The UK pensions environment has been bedevilled by frequent, often very significant changes of policy where one government has overturned the decisions of its predecessor. At the recent general election, for example, the Conservative Party made a virtue out of its proposals to significantly change each of the first tier, means tested and tax incentive elements of the pensions system. Regardless of the merits of the particular proposals, it cannot be good for long-term savers if they face uncertainty of this kind at every election.

Public confidence in the pensions system has been severely shaken over the past twenty years. The Conservative governments of the 1980s drastically cut the value of state pensions, and personal pensions were introduced by a rash of mis-selling scandals. More recently high profile defaults, lower equity returns and the closure of defined benefit occupation schemes have taken the shine off funded pensions also. Any reform of the pensions system now needs to restore some of this lost confidence and must be seen as a credible, durable settlement.

If consensus is required for successful reform, the next questions we must ask are what kind of consensus is required, how much agreement is necessary, and between whom? The ultimate arbiter of political success is the public, and their collective consent is thus the most important form of consensus in this process. Not only is it individuals who finally cast their votes to elect or reject prospective governments, but it is individuals who will ultimately bear the costs of any reform.

Households finally bear the burden of all domestic taxes, gross wages adjust to accommodate changes in employer pension contributions, and individuals are the ones who may have to save more or extend their working lives. Achieving sufficient, and sufficiently durable, consent among the voting public is the key to politically successful pension reform. The questions 'does it work for me?' 'what do I get for what I put in it' 'is it fair to me and to others' 'does it support me to do the right thing' 'does it reward responsibility and discourage irresponsibility' 'do I understand it' are likely to be among the critical factors in sustaining consensus as a new system comes into operation.

However, the public are not the immediate location of the pensions debate. Rather it is the expert and representative groups including pensioner, employee, employer and industry bodies, independent and academic experts who are the direct interlocutors of government in the process of reform. Their actions and pronouncements are very important in shaping public opinion. This pamphlet includes responses from representatives of five important groups—the CBI, the TUC, Scottish Widdows, the National Association of Pension Funds and the Pension Policy Institute. From their responses we can identify where consensus exists and can be built upon, and where it is lacking and needs to be developed.

Perhaps the most difficult group among whom to achieve consensus are the political parties themselves. Pensions were a particularly contentious issue in the 2005 general election, where pensioners accounted for the bulk of the Conservative party's flagship proposals for £4 billion of tax cuts. Pensioners themselves, who are a growing share of the electorate and have a higher than average propensity to vote, have become a key electoral battleground. There is no point in pretending that the political parties will stop competing for this constituency in the service of achieving a stable pensions system for the UK.

Meanwhile the UK has not demonstrated much of a tradition of political consensus over the last thirty years, particularly in relation to pensions policy. In part this is due to our 'winner takes all' constitutional arrangements and their political party counterpart, the 'oppositions oppose' mentality.

There will always be an incentive for political parties to oppose the proposals of their opponents—the government will still get their way and it gives the opposition room to manoeuvre later on if things go wrong. However, it is worth recognising some remarkable elements of stability in the UK's political system. Key elements of the welfare state have survived the last 50 years, including treatment in the NHS according to need and free at the point of delivery; universal education that has steadily extended in scope; and the principle of financial equalisation across local authorities with different needs and tax bases.

Some more recent but apparently durable policy innovations are also instructive. It is hard to see any future government repealing the key elements of the 1980s trades union reforms or re-nationalising the privatised utilities. It is hard to see any future government bringing interest rate decisions back under direct political control, or being elected on the basis of repealing the Human Rights Act. None of these are durable because of any special constitutional arrangements, rather they are durable because they represent the outcome of arguments that have been conclusively and publicly won. The reason why the NHS is hard to touch is because it is so widely valued by the British people, not because health experts agree that it is the best possible system.

These examples are also instructive because in each case there are still people who reject the new status quo. Consensus does not have to be universal to be effective. This is worth considering in relation to the case of pensions. If government waited until there was total consensus on reform, it would have to wait forever. A key issue for the government is thus to decide on which elements of pension reform it requires consensus, and how complete it requires this consensus to be.

So how do we get from here to sufficient consensus to sustain a new pensions settlement? Firstly, there must be sufficient parties to the debate who want to reach a consensus, and who recognise that this is likely to involve compromise from all sides. The second step is for the expert and representative groups to consider their priorities and therefore what trade-offs they are prepared to accept in order to achieve their most important goals. Some organisations are already doing this, but others have a wish list of proposals without any obvious order of priorities. The third step is for government to bring the stakeholder groups together to try and achieve consensus on a limited set of key issues which can act as the durable foundation of a new pensions settlement. We believe there are two key elements that could form such a foundation—agreement on the role of the basic pension and the means of funding it; and agreement on the role of the state in relation to second pensions.

A central conclusion of this pamphlet, and a crucial building block for consensus, is that the first tier pension provided by the state should take people out of poverty without the need for means-tested top ups. A large majority of the expert and representative bodies, including all of the respondents to this pamphlet, support the principle of a universal first tier state pension which prevents pensioner poverty in this way. As well as being supported by a very wide range of expert stakeholders, it would also be in tune with public expectations.

However, such a reform would be hugely ambitious. It would be very expensive, and there is little consensus on how to fund it. A key issue for all parties is thus: what are they prepared to accept as the trade-off for a

## The first tier pension, or the basic pension provided by the state

Throughout this pamphlet we refer to the 'first tier pension' or equivalently the 'basic pension'. This is the pension provided by the state as the foundation for pensioner incomes. At the moment in the UK this is the Basic State Pension. However, a reformed first tier or basic pension could be very different from the existing Basic State Pension, which is a contributory benefit set at a particular level and paid on a particular basis related to each individual's National Insurance contributions history. For 2005/06 the Basic State Pension is £82.05 per week for a single pensioner with at least 44 qualifying years of National Insurance contributions.

To indicate that the first tier could be significantly different from the existing Basic State Pension and paid on a different basis, we refer instead to the 'first tier' or 'basic pension'. The choice between a contributory and citizenship pension is briefly discussed in this pamphlet but, although this is an important issue, we believe it is secondary to our central concerns.

decent first tier? The options are relatively clear, being some mix of: increased taxes or National Insurance contributions; the diversion of other state pensions spending (such as the State Second Pensions, the associated rebates and tax reliefs); the diversion of other government spending; and longer working lives.

The second is achieving consensus on the role of the state in providing or supporting second pensions. Here there are two basic options: either for the state to largely withdraw from the support of second pensions and to redirect the resources into an adequate basic pension; or for the state to provide an adequate basic pension and in addition to provide significant support for second pension saving. The next section addresses the arguments on either side in more depth.

One of the most successful actions of the 1997 Labour Government was to grant operational independence to the Bank of England. Is there any parallel opportunity to remove aspects of pensions policy from the political sphere? It is worth initially making a three-fold distinction between the processes of achieving consensus, of choosing the structure and parameters for the new system, and of implementing decisions.

Government could potentially do a number of things to 'contract out' the process of achieving consensus over pension reform. It is already supporting an independent body (the Pensions Commission) to clarify the factual issues relating to pension reform. It could also bring together key stakeholders in a formal setting to try and achieve consensus on specific issues such as the two we identify above. It could even appoint an agent to do this, for example by requesting a subset of the representative bodies to organise this process. It would be useful for stakeholders to comment publicly on these issues now, so that the government can consider its options.

Government can never contract out the process of actually making the key policy decisions over the structure and parameters of a reformed system, because it will always be ultimately responsible for the results. It is possible to imagine what this process would look like (set up a convention on the future of the UK pensions system and commit in advance to accepting the resulting proposal…) but no one is seriously suggesting this course of action.

Implementing reform is a different matter. Many aspects of the pension system currently require regular review, for example the level of the Basic State Pension, the level of the Pension Credit thresholds, and the various other pension benefits. Others which are not regularly reviewed, such as the state pension age, might benefit from the introduction of regular reviews. Some aspects of the system, for example the value of the contracted out rebate which is calculated by the Government Actuary's Department, are already somewhat removed from the political process.

In some cases it would be possible for government to set out the parameters for policy and then leave implementation to an operationally independent body. For example, if the first tier of state pension provision were to be set at the level required to prevent poverty amongst all of its recipients, then it would be possible to delegate the decision over the precise level. To return to the example of the Bank of England: The Bank is not totally independent, rather it has operational independence to use a prescribed range of monetary policy tools to achieve the inflation target that is set by government. It would be useful for stakeholders to comment on which aspects of the implementation of pensions policy, if any, they think it would be appropriate for government to delegate to an independent agency or agencies.

A further positive example is the Minimum Wage Commission, established by the Government to take the political heat out of the need to strike the right balance between the desire to increase the value of the minimum and the necessity of limiting untoward impacts on the labour market. In this case, Government has retained the right the reject the Commission's recommendations though the cost of doing so would be high.

There is a further powerful reason for introducing a strong element of independent oversight and management into the pension system. In this pamphlet we call for a revitalised first tier state pension. Not long ago, such a proposal would have been strongly criticised on the grounds of public credibility. Just a few years previously, the Thatcher Government had wrecked cross-party consensus on the basic state pensions. It was widely argued that no one would ever believe in the state again and that private funded pensions were the future.

Today, however, faith in that kind of provision has also been undermined by the collapse of a succession of occupational schemes, the lingering effects of personal pension mis-selling and overcharging and the impact of stock market falls on investment values. No type of pension now commands strong public confidence. It is only if the new pension framework is placed firmly in the hands on an independent body that there is any real prospect of rebuilding public confidence in any part of the system

The window of opportunity for serious pension reform in the UK is now open. Inevitably, government has the leading and most onerous role. It not only determines the process by which decisions are reached, it has to decide when sufficient consensus has been achieved, formalise and implement its proposals, and then bear the consequences. Nonetheless, it is not the only actor with responsibilities.

Most of those who have commented on the pensions landscape in the UK have expressed dissatisfaction with the status quo and have put forward their own proposals for reform. All of these now need to commit to the process of achieving sufficient consensus to make reform politically possible in the short term and politically sustainable in the long term. This will mean considering carefully their priorities and the issues on which they are prepared to compromise. They also need to consider what is the best process by which they can achieve consensus. At the end of the day, if a programme of reform is to be successfully implemented and sustained it will require a critical mass of trusted expert and representative bodies to provide vocal commitment and support. In the long term, the stability of pensions policy requires deep rooted public consent of the kind that has sustained the NHS over more than fifty years. Whatever the institutional arrangements for implementing pensions policy, there is no other guarantee of success.

# 3 | The Key Issues: what are the options and where do the stakeholders stand?

## State pensions—first tier reform

If there is one area where strong consensus exists outside government about the need for significant reform, it is in relation to the state pension system. Since the Pensions Green Paper of 2002, which was almost silent on the issue, there has been a significant change in the apparent willingness of government to engage in this debate. Indeed, in February 2005 the DWP published a document called 'Principles for reform—the national pensions debate' which suggested that reform of the state pension system is very much back on the agenda:

> The Government's reforms have significantly improved the outcomes for today's pensioners. However, changes in society mean that we cannot necessarily rely on the existing structures to provide the same outcomes as we move further into the twenty-first century.
>
> DWP, 2005

There is a remarkable degree of consensus about some of the problems with state pension provision in the UK. No-one believes that the current system of state provision represents an unsustainable burden on the public finances, even in the relatively long term. Almost everyone agrees that the prominent role played by means-tested benefits for pensioners causes significant problems in terms of take-up, savings incentives and the overall complexity of the system. Many agree that reform of the first tier of pension provision in the UK—currently the Basic State Pension—is the single most important possible reform for the system as a whole.

## The basic pension should prevent poverty without recourse to means-testing

There is a clear front-running candidate for a reform of the first tier of state pension provision. Analysis by the Pensions Policy Institute of pension reform proposals put forward by 30 organisations shows that 25 of these believe that the first tier should deliver an income that prevents pensioner poverty without the need for means tested top ups. This is approximately equivalent to the Guarantee Credit level within the Pension Credit, currently £109.45 for a single pensioner per week. Almost all of those in favour of first tier provision at this level also support indexation in line with average earnings, to prevent its value falling back below the poverty line.

This reform would remove the need for much, but not all, of the means testing of pensioners required by the current system of state pensions. Just under half of pensioner households were entitled to some Pension Credit in 2004/05. If the government continues to uprate the Basic State Pension and Pension Credit thresholds in manner it has done recently, then by 2025/26 this figure will rise to nearly 2/3 of all pensioner households.[1] If the first tier of state pension provision was increased to the adequacy level then the Pension Credit would become largely redundant. It would be limited to a small minority (principally those without entitlement to the first tier pension and very limited additional savings), the pensions system would become significantly simpler, and incentives would be improved for lower to middle income earners.

Improving the basic pension so that Pension Credit became largely unnecessary would significantly improve incentives for saving. Each additional £1 of private pensioner income currently reduces entitlement

22

## The Basic State Pension and the Pension Credit

The Basic State Pension is currently the first tier of pension provision in the UK. The full Basic State Pension will be £82.05 per week for a single person for the year 2005/06, and is a contributory benefit paid on the basis of National Insurance Contributions. The Basic State Pension is currently significantly below the official poverty line of 60 per cent of contemporary median income.

The Pension Credit, which is means tested rather than a contributory benefit, guarantees a minimum income to those over the age of 60 of £109.45 per week for a single person. This is known as the Guarantee Credit level, and is approximately at the official poverty line. For a single person over the age of 65, with a full Basic State Pension and no other income, the Pension Credit thus provides a maximum benefit of £27.40 per week (£109.45 − £82.05 = £27.40). Each additional £1 of private income then reduces entitlement to Pension Credit by 40 pence. Thus single people over 65 with a full Basic State Pension and a second pension of up to £68.50 per week are entitled to some Pension Credit (£27.40 / 0.4 = £68.50).

to Pension Credit by 40 pence (up to a ceiling where no Pension Credit is payable). However, Housing Benefit and Council Tax Benefit currently present similar incentive problems for pensioners (and for working people also). Pension Credit does not therefore cause all of the existing incentive problems, but a reform that addressed it would be an important move in the right direction.

At the same time we must not overstate or misrepresent the disincentive effect provided by the Pension Credit. There is little evidence that people consciously change their savings behaviour as a result of its existence—that would require very sophisticated individual calculations. However it does make it very difficult for government, financial advisors and product providers to give a clear message about the benefit of saving. It also contributes to a climate in which the public are uncertain about the benefits of saving and resentfully believe that the system punishes those who do save. We should try to secure decent pensioner incomes through rights accrued before retiring rather than through means-tested adjustments after retirement.

It is worth dwelling for a moment on the extent and the importance of the consensus around achieving an adequate non-means tested first tier. There is much more agreement about the right level of generosity for the first tier of state pension provision than there is about how to pay for it, or about its exact form, or about how to make the transition to a new system. However, the breadth of the coalition in favour of the basic proposal is remarkable. It includes the CBI, the TUC, the National Association of Pension Funds, numerous financial service providers, and many pensioner representative groups. Increasing the generosity of first tier provision addresses key objectives for each of these and does not run against the interests of any of them.

In isolation, a reform that increased the generosity of first tier pension provision would give relatively more to those who are not currently receiving means tested benefits. However, the overall impact of pension reform depends just as much on the distribution of the burdens as it does on the distribution of the benefits. A pensions reform that increased the generosity of the first tier would not necessarily be regressive overall if it was funded in the right way. The improvement in the basic state pension rights of those on the highest incomes can be fairly balanced with a restructuring of state support for second pension provision. It would, however, be politically impossible to remove accrued rights to state second pensions and politically extremely difficult to offset any such rights against improved first tier provision.

It is also important to recognise that targeting spending on lower income groups via means testing is not necessarily the best solution to the particular challenges facing our pensions system. Policies which give more help to those on lower incomes are an important tool for achieving social justice, but they are not appropriate in all cases. We do not means test hospital services, for example, even though it would be more fiscally progressive to do so.

## Funding reform

Perhaps the most difficult question is how to pay for a more generous first tier state pension. State spending on UK pension benefits accounted for 5.1 per cent of GDP in 2004/05, and under current government projections this is expected to rise to 5.6 per cent in 2054/55.[2] According to the Pensions Commission, increasing the Basic State Pension to the level of the Guarantee Credit, maintaining it there by indexing it to earnings, and ending the contribution requirements would cost in the region of an additional 3.8 per cent of GDP at the end of this period. This would represent a two-thirds increase in state pension spending as a proportion of GDP at a cost of roughly £44 billion in 2004 terms. These are clearly enormous sums, although as we have already pointed out, a significant increase in the proportion of national wealth going to pensions will have to take place simply to meet the rising proportion of the population that will be retired.

If this option were to be pursued then the funding options are essentially to increase taxation or National Insurance contributions; to divert public expenditure either from other pension uses or from non-pension uses; or to increase the age from which the first tier pension is payable. There is no clear consensus about the solution to this problem. It is, however, possible to say something about the politics of each option.

Increasing taxation or National Insurance contributions would be the most direct, and perhaps the most politically difficult, way of funding an enhanced first tier state pension. In many ways, if pension reform is funded via increased public revenues then National Insurance contributions rather than taxation are the most likely vehicle. There has long been a perplexing distinction between the relative public acceptability of raising additional National Insurance contributions and the high level of public sensitivity to the headline rates of income tax. It has the further benefit of not placing the tax costs of higher pensioners on pensioners themselves. In addition, the principle of hypothecation appears to strike a chord with the public, and National Insurance contributions are at least officially ring-fenced to pay principally for state pensions. At this stage, however the likelihood of some additional NI or tax to pay for improved state pensions must be acknowledged.

A key issue for the stakeholders to this debate is thus to consider: if additional public revenue is to be raised for first tier state pension reform, then how exactly is this to be done and via what instruments? If National Insurance contributions are to be the mechanism, then what is the appropriate balance between employee and employer contributions? Should all earnings above the lower earnings limit be included, as they were in 2002?

The other potential sources of funding for such a reform of the first tier are to push back the average age at which the state pension becomes payable, and to find other items of public expenditure which can be curtailed. The pension age issue is dealt with in more detail below. In relation to other areas of public expenditure, the first possibility to rule out is that pension reform can be funded from efficiency savings elsewhere in government—the numbers involved are simply of a different order. In many areas of the public services (such as health care) efficiency savings are only likely to contribute to restraining the growth of costs. Demographic shifts that reduce the proportion of young people in the population may reduce some spending pressures, but is difficult to imagine reducing the proportion of GDP spent on the major public services such as health, education or protective services in order to fund pension reform.

It is not possible to fund the necessary reform through changes in the state pension age alone. According to the Pension Commission, even if the Pension Credit and State Second Pension were abolished, a first tier non-contributory pension at the level of the Guarantee Credit would still require the state pension age to rise to 72 (for men and women) if the aim was to keep state pension expenditure at the 5.7 per cent of GDP envisaged under current government spending plans for 2043/44.

Another candidate is the rest of the state pension system. Payments of SERPS and the State Second Pension accounted for 0.6 per cent of GDP in 2004/05 and are projected to rise to 1.8 per cent by 2054/55.[3] National

Insurance rebates accounted for 0.9 per cent of GDP in 2004/05 and are expected to fall to 0.4 per cent of GDP in 2050/51.[4] Tax relief on private pension saving represented foregone public revenues equivalent to another 1.8 per cent of GDP (more than £19 billion) in 2003/04.[5] Ending provision of the second tier and redirecting the resources would thus make a very substantial contribution to the costs of reforming the first tier. Of course, the full impact could only be enjoyed in the longer term as there cannot be any question of removing pension rights that have already been accrued.

The pros and cons of this approach, and the degree of consensus around the idea of using National Insurance rebates and reform of tax reliefs at least in part to fund first tier pensions, are discussed in more detail below.

## Should the basic pension be a contributory benefit or paid on the basis of residency?

A final issue in relation to the first tier of state pension provision is whether it should be contributory or residence based. Our current first tier pension—the Basic State Pension—is a contributory benefit paid on the basis of individuals being credited with sufficient National Insurance contributions. The alternative would be to move towards a citizen's pension —a benefit paid solely on the basis of a residency test. The two key benefits of a residency based first tier pension are that it is beneficial to women, whose working careers are more likely to be interrupted by caring responsibilities, and it is administratively simpler than a contributory system. The key benefit of a contributory system is that, as with hypothecation, it appears to strike a chord with the public who feel that they are 'putting something in to get something out'. A contributory pension might also recognise longer working lives such as those of people who enter the workforce earlier rather than continuing in further or higher education.

At present there does not appear to be a consensus on this issue. Some groups such as the National Association of Pension Funds are strongly in favour of a citizen's pension, others like the CBI support the status quo, and many others have either not expressed a view or have said the issue needs further consideration. Alan Johnson made it clear when he was Secretary of State for Work and Pensions that he was interested in exploring the matter in greater depth. Public sensitivity over immigration may be an unwelcome and relevant factor in this debate, especially if it is proposed to change the criteria for receiving the first tier pension so as to significantly benefit those who have immigrated to the UK later in their working lives. In fact it is hard to image that a shift from contributions to residency criteria could do otherwise, as 44 years of contributions are currently required for a full National Insurance contributions record.

There is the added complication that a change to a citizenship pension in the near future would create many anomalies between those who worked in the past and paid a full 'stamp', those who paid a lower contribution and those who chose not to work at all. Nothing poisons welfare reform more than the sense that the rules have been re-written to dis-advantage those who tried to make the best provision for themselves.

As with any policy that affects a large number of people, there are political dangers in changing the status quo first tier pension, and reform would require a compelling case in its favour. It is prudent to assume that with any major policy change affecting incomes the losers will make significantly more noise than the winners. A major reform would thus have to clear a high hurdle before receiving political commitment. Reform could be derailed by relatively minor drawbacks, even if overall the policy would be better for the majority of people, and even if the status quo has larger drawbacks. The benefits thus have to be very clear cut—and seen to be so in the public domain—before a major reform could be implemented.

# State pensions—second tier reform

First tier state pension reform is a key part of the pensions puzzle, but it is far from being the only important issue. A second tier of state pension benefits providing an income related top up to the Basic State Pension has been a feature of the UK pensions landscape since 1961. The system of tax relief for pension contributions is another element of state support for second pensions that has recently received relatively little attention. The nature and extent of state support for second pensions is key.

At the moment there is very limited consensus in relation to second tier state pension provision in the UK. Most but not all commentators think that the state should continue to support second pensions, but that the way in which it does so should be reformed. A significant group including the NAPF and the British Chambers of Commerce are in favour of abolition to fund first tier reform. However another group including the TUC and CBI are in favour of retaining and reforming the second tier. It is important for all parties to the pensions debate to indicate their views of the second tier, rebates and tax relief in the current system, and most importantly to recognise the trade-offs that their views entail. Achieving consensus around reform of the second tier in the UK is a critical step on the way to achieving consensus overall.

## Pros and cons of state support for second pensions

A first choice then, is whether the state should provide any support for second pension saving at all. If the state withdrew from such support it could concentrate the significant resources currently used for this purpose on an adequate basic pension. As well as being affordable, such a system would have the important virtue clarity and simplicity. The purpose of state pensions would become to prevent poverty and leave the individuals to make their own arrangements for income replacement. A state pension system which consisted only of an adequate (poverty prevention) first tier would present individuals with a very clear picture of their responsibilities.

The simple state system that only provided a first tier pension also avoids the state needing to take decisions about the appropriate level of second tier provision. Many of the complexities of our current system stem from different decisions that have been taken over the years about the replacement rate the second pensions should provide, the desire to balance future state and funded provision, and the appropriate balance between state and individual responsibility. A system where the state pension simply prevents poverty avoids these complications.

However, even with an enhanced basic pension many people might expect the state to continue to assist in the provision or at least the funding of their second pension. There is a particularly strong case for helping people who may find it difficult to make pension savings because they are on modest incomes, but for whom a pension of £109.45 per week would represent a poor proportion of their typical earnings. It would be politically very difficult to withdraw the State Second Pension which has been introduced precisely to assist this group and those whose working lives are interrupted by caring responsibilities without making some other provision to fulfil its role.

There are a number of other arguments in favour of the state providing an income related second tier pension. The first is that individuals may not make rational decisions about their own savings behaviour and thus need to be compelled via a state second tier pension to act in their own best interests. Many people who are faced with complex and long term decisions simply put off making any choice at all. However, in the case of private pensions this implies not beginning to save.

There is also evidence that many people discount future income relative to current consumption at a very high rate. In the case of pensions this implies not saving enough. The state may thus have a role in preventing 'disappointment' among pensioners as well as technical poverty. A key test of pension reform is that it must enable, but not ensure, that most people can achieve reasonable replacement rates. The government will have to be able to say what level of savings this will

## The purpose of the second state pension

The Basic State Pension is now below the poverty line, and the latest incarnation of the state second tier—the State Second Pension introduced in 2002—is expected to become a flat rate benefit in around 30-40 years time as a result of linking the Upper Earnings Limit for National Insurance contributions to prices rather than earnings. When the State Second Pension was introduced there were proposals to bring this transition forward, but these have not been pursued by government. These two flat rate pensions will then add up to an income sufficient to take their recipient just above the poverty line. Pension Credit will then provide an additional benefit of up to 60 per cent of the value of the State Second Pension. Pensioners without a full Basic State Pension—including many women—will find that some of their State Second Pension will not qualify for Pension Credit, as the Savings Credit is only applied to income above the level of the Basic State Pension. Private pension income will also reduce the amount of Pension Credit received.

The State Second Pension is thus intended to fulfil a very different function from its predecessor, the State Earnings Related Pension Scheme, which was intended to provide an earnings-related addition to an adequate Basic State Pension. Now the State Second Pension plus the Basic State Pension plus the Pension Credit are expected to collectively ensure that their recipients are above the poverty line. For the first time since 1961 the state is effectively withdrawing from earnings-related income replacement for pensioners.

require in addition to state pension benefits, and the public will have to feel that this is reasonable and achievable for them.

For some people at least, the government is also a more attractive provider of financial products. Despite their low level of current take up, stakeholder pensions do offer a relatively low cost personal pension product. However, they are only low cost in comparison to many previous personal pensions. Their administration costs are still high relative to most occupational schemes and even higher in relation to state administered schemes which do not have to incur the costs of persuading people to join. Stakeholder charges are currently capped at one per cent of the fund value each year and some providers are lobbying to increase this limit. The Government Actuary's Department Survey of Occupational Pensions Schemes in 2000 measured the average private sector occupational scheme cost at 0.4 per cent of managed funds per year. The annual administrative cost of the National Insurance fund is approximately 0.1 per cent of the value of the accrued rights.

## Principles for reforming state support for second pensions

Any state support for second pensions should meet some key tests. It should enable most people to retire on a reasonable proportion of their working income. It should clearly incentivise personal responsibility and saving. It should target more support on those people with low incomes who find it difficult to make additional savings, including carers and others with intermittent working lives. Most importantly of course, it should be seen to be fair.

If the basic pension were adequate to prevent poverty, it would become much easier to reform state support for second pension saving in a way which passed these tests. The value of such support could be deployed through a matching scheme which offered clear incentives to make pension savings—for each £1 of private saving the state could add £x. The rate of matching could be higher for people on low incomes. The total amount available to each individual would be limited, perhaps via an annual cap on support or via a cap applying to a longer period to allow for varying circumstances such as a period of unemployment or caring. There could even be credits for circumstances like caring responsibilities. It would not ensure a given replacement rate, but would assist and enable individuals in achieving this for themselves.

We would envisage the Government setting out clearly its aims for second pensions. It would be explicit about the level of contribution it was prepared to make and the level of contribution it was assuming from individuals and/or their employers. It would exemplify, for example, what level of replacement income it would expect someone on a given income to accrue in return for a certain level of employee or employer contribution. In contrast to the obscurity and complexity of the current system a new approach to government support for second pensions would need to be simple, understandable and clear about personal responsibilities and incentives.

## Funding again

It is vitally important to be clear about the costs of pension reform. It is not possible to bring the first tier state pension up to the adequacy level and to retain the second tier at its currently planned level without significant increases in taxes or National Insurance contributions. As discussed earlier, efficiency savings, reductions in non-pension spending, and even changes in the state pension age are very unlikely to be sufficient in themselves. It does not make sense to rule out on a point of principle any increase in tax or National Insurance rates to help pay for pension reform. Nonetheless, there are significant resources available within the pension system to facilitate reform.

Tax relief on pensions saving currently represents foregone public revenue equivalent to 1.8 per cent of GDP. This is a very substantial sum, for example sufficient to increase state spending on the Basic State Pension by 50 per cent. Higher earners with higher tax rates benefit disproportionately from the current system. Out of 35 million people of working age, 2.5 million higher rate tax payers get 55 per cent of the value of all tax relief on pension saving. 13 million basic rate tax payers share the other 45 per cent, and nine million other taxpayers receive nothing.[6] This is grossly unfair, and the value of these reliefs should also be considered as part of the resources available for a wide-ranging reform of the pensions system.

The government has introduced a new life-time cap on the value of an individual's pension fund contributions that can be tax advantaged.

This is a worthwhile move in the right direction. However, the system remains overwhelmingly favourable to higher earners and the new cap does nothing to improve the incentives for lower income savers. Nonetheless it opens the door to more far reaching reform.

Tinkering with tax reliefs for pension contributions has often been regarded—with good reason—as politically very hazardous. On the other hand, the gross disparity with which the Government currently spends the largest part of £20bn a year on a small minority of the population is hard to defend if we are looking for radical and sustainable reform of the system. Doing so could make a significant contribution to the type of £1 for £1 incentive scheme for second pension savings that we have outlined above. Although further analysis is required, it is likely that many tax payer, including the majority of higher rate taxpayers could gain could gain significantly from such an approach.

As indicated earlier, SERPS and the State Second Pension accounted for 0.6 per cent of GDP in 2004/05 and are projected to rise to 1.8 per cent by 2054/55. Few people would argue that the State Second Pension is a bad thing in itself. It has improved the generosity of the pension system for low income individuals and those with working histories that are interrupted by caring responsibilities. However, there are still major gaps in its coverage—5 million men and 4 million women out of 35 million working age people are not accruing entitlements.[7] The key question to ask is whether the resources directed at the State Second Pension could be better used on other pension spending.

## Contracted out National Insurance rebates

If accruals to the State Second Pension were ended to help pay for first tier reform, the associated rebates would probably have to go too, as the rebates only exist to compensate individuals for their decision to opt out of receiving it in retirement. The financial benefit of ending accruals is of course only felt some years later, at the time the pension would have been paid. The financial benefit of ending rebates would be felt imme-

## Contracting out and National Insurance rebates

The UK is almost unique in having 'contracting-out' as part of its pensions system, which adds a significant layer of complexity to the savings environment. Contracting out allows individuals to choose not to accrue entitlements to the State Second Pension and instead to have the Inland Revenue pay a compensating rebate into a private or occupational pension. The rebate is meant to accurately reflect the value of the foregone state pension benefit. Private and occupational pension schemes are thus compensated by the rebates at a level expected to generate the benefits they must pay out in return.

If contracting out were abolished now, and all those currently receiving rebates were brought back into the State Second Pension, then no-one should be worse off because the rebates are supposed to represent fair value for the benefits foregone. If state second pensions and the rebates disappeared at the same time as a wider reform then the picture is less simple. Contracted-out individuals would then be giving up their rebates in exchange for whatever they gained from the new system (e.g. a higher first tier state pension). Contracted-in individuals would be giving up their state second pensions on the same basis.

diately. The rebates account for approximately one quarter of the total flow of saving into private pension funds, and were 0.9 per cent of GDP in 2004/05, although their total value is expected to fall in the future.

If pensioners are to avoid becoming poorer relative to the rest of society, then the total flow of resources to pensioners must increase. Increasing state pension resources purely at the expense of private pension resources would fail to address this issue. The UK pensions system will continue to require a healthy private pensions sector regardless of reform to the state sector, so any reform which affects the rebates must allow the private sector to play its role effectively.

Private pension schemes are only compensated by the rebates at a level expected to generate the benefits they must pay out in return. The key benefit to the schemes is thus the additional volume of funds, which may lead to lower administration costs and therefore higher effective returns for savers. Another possible benefit is the extent to which individuals are encouraged by the existence of the rebates to make additional contributions of their own. Unfortunately it is not yet really clear how significant these two issues are, and further evidence is needed. It is worth noting, however, that the National Association of Pension Funds (NAPF), which represents the major occupational pension scheme providers, has adopted the clear position that losing the rebates is a price worth paying for effective reform of the first tier, as their response at the end of this pamphlet makes clear.

Ending the rebates would certainly have an impact on occupational pension provision. Occupational schemes which are contracted out, including most if not all defined benefit schemes, would either have to adjust their level of benefits downwards, or would require additional contributions from their members. However, if contracting out were abolished but state second pensions remained, then once again individuals should be no better or worse off. Only the composition, and not the level, of their retirement income would change. If the state second tier and the rebates were replaced in a wider reform then once again the gains and losses would depend on the details of the proposal. Some companies might take the opportunity to switch from defined benefit to defined contribution schemes and claim that this was because of a change to the rebates system. It would need to be very clear to all parties what the real impact on occupational schemes of changes to the rebates would be.

Similarly careful account would need to be taken of any unintended consequences of reforming tax reliefs to achieve a more coherent and fairer system of incentives for pension savings. Overall, the effect should me to draw more people into pensions savings. But there would be some individuals would chose to make their long-term savings in other ways and it would be important to ensure that there was not major impact on employer pension schemes.

## Compulsion and incentives for employees and employers

The independent Pensions Commission was originally set up to keep under review the regime for private pensions and long-term saving in the UK, and

> On the basis of [its] assessment of how effectively the current voluntarist approach is developing over time, to make recommendations to the Secretary of State for Work and Pensions on whether there is a case for moving beyond the current voluntarist approach.
>
> Pensions Green Paper 2002

It was quickly nicknamed 'the compulsion commission', and the issue of compulsion in the UK pensions system shot up the policy and political agenda.

The first point to make in respect of compulsion is that it is a second order issue. A given level of compulsion in the pensions system is only a means to various ends, such as increased overall savings rates or a more equal distribution of pensioner incomes. Compulsion is a significant part of the puzzle, but it should not be the exclusive focus of the wider discussion around pensions policy. The Pensions Commission itself has taken the lead in broadening the debate in a helpful way.

Unfortunately, and despite the best efforts of the Commission, the debate around compulsion remains bedevilled with confusion. There are many different aspects of pension provision to which compulsion by government either does or could exist, and it is not always clear what is being referred to in general discussions of 'voluntarism' and 'compulsion'. Individuals could be compelled to join and contribute to various types of schemes, employers could be compelled to establish or contribute to various types of scheme, and financial service providers could be compelled to comply with a range of regulatory and legislative requirements. It is no good talking about compulsion without being clear what kind of compulsion is under consideration.

**37**

The debate around compulsion has focused on the issues of whether individuals should be compelled to save more of their income, and whether employers should be compelled to offer or contribute to a scheme for their employees. There is, of course, already a very significant degree of compulsion on individuals to make provision for their retirement. Once over the Lower Earnings Limit all employees are required to contribute both to the Basic State Pension and to some form of second pension, either via the State Second Pension or via contracting out into a private or occupational scheme. Employers, on the other hand, are not required either to offer or to contribute to a pension scheme although they contribute, of course, to the National Insurance system.

It may be helpful to discuss the different issues that are involved in extending compulsion for individuals and for employers.

## Individuals

Currently there is no compulsion on individuals to make private savings at all. Those who remain opted into the State Second Pension are not required to make any additional provision. At first sight introducing this kind of compulsion may seem attractive, on the logic that individuals will eventually benefit from the savings they are required to make. However, at present many people on lower to middle incomes face relatively poor incentives to save, partly because their own private saving is likely to reduce their entitlement to Pension Credit.

Indeed, there is a high level of expert consensus that it would be difficult to increase the existing level of compulsion on individuals to make pension provision when means testing in retirement is expected to be so extensive. Under the current pensions system, more than two thirds of the pensioner population is expected to be entitled to the Pension Credit by 2040. All of these people will be experiencing benefit withdrawal as a result of making private savings and a substantial number would see there forced additional savings merely reduce the gap between the basic state pension and the Minimum Income Guarantee. Forcing people to increase their level of savings when they would see little or nothing in return would be politically very dangerous indeed.

Introducing individual compulsion becomes much more plausible if the requisite first tier reform has addressed the incentive problems currently created by the Pension Credit. Individuals would then at least see more of the benefit of the savings they were forced to make.

On the other hand, a number of further questions then arise. What is the right level of compulsion on individuals? What principles would inform such a decision? Should the level vary across an individual's life-course to take account of issues like saving for the deposit on a first home, or raising a family? Should it be possible to set off higher saving in one period against lower saving in another? What interaction would compulsion have with levels of voluntary saving? Most fundamentally, if the first tier of state provision effectively prevents pensioner poverty and there are good incentives to save at all income levels, what is the argument for additional individual compulsion in any case?

There is one group of individuals for whom further compulsion to make pension provision might be appropriate: the self-employed. At present self employed people are required to make flat rate National Insurance Contributions and in exchange gain entitlement to the Basic State Pension but not the State Second Pension. Many self-employed people are engaged in relatively low paid work and are unlikely to be making significant private savings. If they do not make additional private pension provision they will thus end up relying on the Guarantee Credit to bring them up to, but not above, the poverty line. The pensions system, with its effective opt-out for the self employed, was established with a model of prosperous, capital owning self-employment in mind. This is no longer reflects the reality for many self-employed people, who should now be brought back within the ambit of the pensions system on the same basis as employees.

## Employers

There is no doubt that the pension system as a whole would be considerably more robust if more employers made more generous pension provision for their employees. Most current trends are in the opposite direction. The private sector is reducing both the value and the security of its pension promise and the public sector is now also seeking to reduce the value of public sector pension provision—in part on the argument that the public sector no longer needs such generous provision when private pensions are being cut back. There are many competitive factors in the labour market nationally and internationally that are also creating pressure to reduce employer provision.

Employer pension provision has always provided a tricky challenge for governments. As essentially private sector activities but with a clear public purpose, governments have struggled to balance the incentives that encourage employers to provide schemes with the security that employees demand. It is worth noting that the decline in employer defined benefit provision has quickened as the level of prudential regulation has risen. As the basic pension has declined in value, second pensions have been required to play an ever greater role in overall pension provision. In turn, governments have been pressed to introduce more regulation and more complex rescue schemes for the rapidly diminishing number of people who have the chance to be in such schemes.

A common response from the trade unions has been to call for employer provision to be made compulsory. For employers currently making pension contributions above the chosen minimum this would not cause any difficulties. For others it would essentially represent a government imposed cost increase (and corresponding employee benefit) unless the companies made corresponding adjustments to take home pay. Unsurprisingly, this option is firmly opposed by employers and their representatives. It is, however, supported by many employee representative groups including the TUC.

At the very least the limits of this approach need to be understood. Any new level of compulsion would inevitably raise costs for some employers—perhaps unsustainably—whilst setting a benchmark well below the level of the best schemes. Those who currently get little or no employer support are likely to be those on lower incomes who have least ability to sacrifice salary for pension contributions. So any increase in employer contributions would have to be incremental and would often seem inadequate. Of course, similar criticisms can be made of the introduction of the Minimum Wage, which is now widely seen as a success. All of this suggests that we should not rule out further employer contributions, but that we should recognise that progress would have to be slow and careful.

Perhaps the least onerous proposal is that where an employer offers an occupational pension scheme, employees could be required to opt out of membership rather than being required to opt in. Evidence from the US suggests that this dramatically increases the proportion of the workforce that are scheme members even after several years. It would represent very little additional compulsion on either employees or employers and there is a good degree of consensus—including among the main employee and employer representative groups—that it would be a sensible change.

What ever is done about compulsion, Governments need to examine how they can create an environment which does more to make employers want to make better pension provision. Defined benefit schemes probably never made strict bottom line business sense, but by becoming an important feature of the labour market, they helped the market economy function more effectively and with greater social support than otherwise would have been possible.

The challenge is to recreate the will amongst employers to shoulder a similar responsibility in a very different economy. This will mean examining both the direct and indirect pressure on business to cut provision. For the defined benefit schemes, having compulsory employee membership will help stem the loss of new funds that can accelerate scheme closure. Regulation needs to be reasonable and light touch—a move than will be easier if the first tier state pension is more generous

41

and reliable. There is a good case for preventing companies that make starkly more generous provision for senior executives gaining any tax assistance to do so.

Another level of compulsion on employers would be to require them to offer a particular form of occupational pension scheme to their employees. For this to have any advantage for the members over an equally generous employer contribution to a private pension, such a scheme would need to either have lower administration costs or pool risk among the members in a similar way that a defined benefit schemes does. Once again, the costs of this option would eventually need to be reflected in gross wages. In addition, employers and especially small employers might find such arrangements inflexible and burdensome.

If all jobs were advertised with their gross remuneration, including the value of employer pension contributions, it might help individuals make better decisions about their employment choices. If prospective employees systematically under-value employer pension contributions, then employers have an incentive not to pay them and to increase take home pay by a lesser amount instead. In addition many public sector jobs would look dramatically more attractive to prospective applicants.

We can reduce if not eliminate the labour market pressure to cut provision. The promised ending of the two tier labour market in the public sector will have its biggest impact if it prevents competition resting on pension costs. The case for bringing the self-employed into the full National Insurance system is strengthened because it will also reduce the tendency to use 'self-employed' contractors to undercut existing pensionable employment. More could also be done—as in the rest of the EU—to ensure that incoming workers from the accession states do not obtain employment purely because of their willingness to accept posts with no pension rights.

Of course, a balance has to be struck with the need for a flexible labour market. Equally, however, there is no point in trying to reconstruct the pension system if wider economic policies are constantly undermining the new provision. We would argue that a close examination of all these issues is at least as important as the discussion of the extension of compulsion to employers.

## Working lives

It is important to be clear about the distinction between the retirement age (when an individual permanently stops working) and the state pension age (when state pension benefits become payable). According to Pension Commission estimates, in 2004 the average retirement age among those who were economically active at 50 was 63.8 years for men, and 61.6 years for women. There is almost universal consensus on the need both to increase the effective retirement age in the UK from its current level closer to the state pension age, and to soften what is currently often a sharp transition from full time work into full time retirement.

Increasing effective retirement ages reduces the cost of pensions because they are paid for a shorter period, and increases the tax revenues and private earnings available to fund pension benefits. Very roughly, each year by which average retirement ages go up reduces the long-term share of GDP required to hold average pensioner incomes stable at their current level by approximately one per cent.[8] Such increases are not only achieved by increasing activity rates among those people below the state pension age. It will also be important to increase activity rates among those over 65 years old.

Where there is much less consensus is on whether to raise the state pension age. There are two fundamental reasons to do so. One is to reduce the overall cost of any given level of state pension benefits, or alternatively to increase the generosity of state pension benefits for any given level of overall cost. The second reason is to encourage people to continue working, thereby contributing to public revenues and their own private savings, whilst at the same time decreasing the period over which their private savings need to last.

Many bodies have brought forward specific proposals for a new state pension age, and there have been a series of newspaper headlines focusing on the age recommended in each case. Much of this has an inappropriate air of urgency, as changes in the state pension age would need to be phased in over a long period. For example, the currently planned increase in the state pension age for women from 60 to 65 will be phased over the ten years from 2010 to 2020.

The first task should be to agree on some principles. It would be possible, for example, to link the state pension age to the length of an individual's working life. If the number of contributory years was increased, but there was no fixed state pension age, the system would show an age bias towards those who start working live younger. This needs more detailed examination, but it might go some way towards meeting the concern that raising the state pension age would disadvantage those who start work younger, and who work in lower paid jobs which in the past have had a lower life expectancy.

This is exactly the kind of area where an independent body could be given the responsibility of administering the policy in the long term once its parameters have been decided by government.

# 4 | Conclusion

The UK's pension system is in need of reform, not because it is in crisis but because it could serve the needs of the public so much better than it does at present. Half a million pensioner households currently live in poverty because they fail to claim their means-tested entitlements. Lower income workers face poor incentives to save, and under current plans means testing will become more and more prevalent in the pensioner population. The system is too complicated, and confidence in both state and private pensions systems is low.

This pamphlet contains a number of specific suggestions for how to deal with these problems. A key conclusion is that we should raise the basic pension provided by the state to the level of the Guarantee Credit (£109.45 for a single person per week in 2005/06) and index it to earnings. We also believe that state support for the second pension saving should be reformed. A reformed system should enable most people to retire on a reasonable proportion of their working income. It should clearly incentivise personal responsibility and saving. It should target more support on those people with low incomes who find it difficult to make additional savings, including carers and others with intermittent working lives. One way to achieve this is via the government matching contributions form employees and employers to their own second pension funds.

Funding reform will mean a significant re-organisation of the very considerable existing state resources devoted to pensions including the

State Second Pension, the associated National Insurance rebates and tax reliefs on pension saving. In addition, the self-employed should be properly brought into the system, and we should not rule out the possibility of future rises in National Insurance contributions to pay for pension reform. We should re-consider the existing tax reliefs on pension saving which disproportionately benefit higher rate tax payers and have little incentive effect for lower earners. The foregone revenue they represent could be much better used.

But the central purpose of this pamphlet is not just to present another set of proposals for a new pensions system in the UK. First and foremost, it is an attempt to move the political debate about pensions forward, and an attempt to show how the necessary consensus can be built. We need enough consensus first of all to enable reform to take place and then to sustain it over the long term.

We believe that consensus can be built around some key issues. There is widespread consensus about the need for the state to provide an adequate first tier pension on the model that we recommend. This can act as the foundation for a wider consensus. The next two issues where consensus is needed are the role of the state in supporting second pension saving and the means of funding the reform package as a whole. Agreement around these issues will provide the structure for a consensus that is sufficiently broad and durable to enable successful reform.

Compulsion is a second order issue compared to these fundamental building blocks for reform. There is already quite strong expert consensus that individuals should be required to opt out of their employer pension scheme rather than opt in as at present. On the other hand there is little consensus about the desirability of additional compulsion on either employers or individuals to contribute to a second pension. With the important exception of bringing the self-employed properly into the National Insurance system, we believe that additional compulsion on individuals would be undesirable in the absence of a reform to the first tier which addressed the current incentive problems.

However, we do not think that additional compulsion to save should be ruled out indefinitely. The time scale of the problems it is meant to address means there should not be an artificial sense of urgency over this issue.

Both government and the expert stakeholders such as employer and employee representatives have responsibilities in the process of achieving consensus. Government needs to focus the debate on the key issues and use its power to bring the stakeholders together to engage constructively with each other. The stakeholders need to commit to a meaningful process of consensus building rather than an endless process of positioning and negotiation. They need to identify their priorities and consider the trade-offs that they are prepared to accept.

The pensions debate needs to change in character, from a competition between interest groups to a process of achieving agreement. If this does not happen then any significant reforms will be difficult or impossible to implement, and even more unlikely to endure. We have tried to show how this shift can be achieved between government and the expert stakeholders. We have also suggested some institutional mechanisms to help prevent a new settlement from being unravelled. But in the longer term, it is only the deep support of the general public that will sustain a pensions consensus over the coming decades. They are the most important constituency, and they are ultimately why the politics of pension reform is just as important as any policy solution, no matter how brilliant.

# Part Two
# Stakeholder Responses

“

# 5 | Digby Jones  CBI

In 2003, the CBI established its Pensions Strategy Group to provide a voice for businesses in the debate over pensions. The group, chaired by Richard Greenhalgh,[9] was made up of senior business leaders from companies in the CBI's membership, and was charged with looking at the future of UK pensions; how employers can improve future pension provision; and what other changes might be needed to the UK's occupational and state pension systems to ensure individuals achieve a decent income in retirement.

The Strategy Group provided a number of key ideas for reform from the employers' perspective. In particular it underlined that:

- while the UK pensions system has served individuals well over the years, a number of reforms will be needed to cope with the challenges ahead;
- reform must be built on a combination of state and private pillars;
- compulsory private pensions will not solve the emerging crisis;
- for the voluntary system to deliver for pensioners, a combination of reforms will be needed;
- individuals will have to save more and employer provision will need to be enhanced;
- the state pension system will need to be reformed;
- individuals will have to work longer.

The CBI believes that UK pension provision should comprise a well-balanced mix of state (pay-as-you-go) and private (funded) systems. Within this, we believe that building on the voluntary approach to private pensions saving is more likely to be successful than the alternative of compulsory contributions to saving schemes.

### Reform the state system

The Government has successfully addressed pensioner poverty by targeting state resources on the poorest pensioners. But there are a number of important concerns that need to be addressed: disincentives for individuals with small amounts of voluntary saving; the complexity of existing arrangements which act as a further deterrent; and the long term growth in the numbers reliant on means tested benefits.

The CBI has recommended that the government take immediate action to remove current disincentives to save. In particular it should permit 'cash conversion' of small pensions saving where the individual would have been better off under state benefits. But over the longer term the CBI recommends that future savings from a rise in the state pension age should be used to raise the level of the basic state pension to the level of the guarantee credit, and that the State Second Pension should be retained.

The CBI believes there is a strong case for the state to continue to provide a second tier earnings related pension for those employers or employees for whom private provision is not appropriate, or who wish to contribute to a top up pension via the state. Even with an enhanced basic state pension, many individuals will not reach the common target replacement rate of between half and two thirds of earnings and therefore need to make additional provision. People should have the option to accrue earnings related pension rights and of doing this via the state. Many SMEs do not have the expertise to get involved in pensions and would wish the state to take responsibility. They recognise that costs may have to rise for employers and employees currently not making top up provision—but a growing number accept that this is a price that may have to be paid.

There may well be a case for reviewing the State Second Pension and moving towards a simplified and perhaps funded state earnings related pensions scheme which enables people to understand their pension entitlement and which commands greater public and political support.

## Compulsion will not solve the emerging crisis

Given that many groups—particularly the TUC—have argued that compulsory employer and employee contributions to private pension schemes are the answer to the emerging pensions crisis, the CBI's Pensions Strategy Group spent a long time considering the potential impact of a compulsory private savings regime in the UK—and it is worth considering how private compulsion would impact on savings and the economy further.

The CBI believes that compulsory private savings would:

• become the norm for contributions rather than the floor upon which all would build. We are particularly concerned that if the rate at which compulsion were set were seen to be the 'right' level at which individuals should save for their retirement, the UK would see an overall reduction in saving for retirement.

• remove freedom of choice from individuals. Depending on their level of income, expenditure and family commitments, individuals may prefer to reduce debts or save in some other way.

• threaten the further erosion of tax incentives which encourage pension provision and further undermine occupational pension provision and pension saving more generally.

• be unaffordable for some employers and employees. The CBI estimates that employer compulsion at a five per cent contribution rate would cost £11bn per annum, while a contribution rate at 10 per cent would cost over £22bn per annum. This would have a damaging effect on many companies, particularly SMEs, by damaging profitability, growth and employment in such companies. While some firms could simply not afford compulsory contributions, there will also be some low-income employees who would not be able to afford new pension contributions.

• lead to distortion of economic activity—making some firms reluctant to grow and hire new employees beyond the minimum threshold for compulsion and leading other firms to move into the black economy.

Evidence from Australia shows that compulsory private provision is not a guaranteed solution to the savings problem. Compulsory private savings were introduced as part of national wage bargaining in 1986 and in 1992 were extended to all employees (not just those covered by wage bargaining settlements). The Superannuation Guarantee instructed employers to contribute to a fund for each of their workers at a rate of four per cent which eventually rose to nine per cent in July 2002: employees agreed that they would receive a lower pay rise in consequence.

Non-compulsory household saving rates in Australia have fallen from nearly 10 per cent in the mid-1970s to 0.5 per cent in 2004. While other factors are likely to have influenced this fall, a recent paper by the Australian Reserve Bank suggests that compulsory superannuation may have increased total household saving by as little as two per cent in recent years. Only high income households tended to make further voluntary contributions to their schemes while younger households tended to take out further credit to maintain spending in the face of nine per cent contributions.

Were the UK to go down this road, the Government could inadvertently signal that a modest level of saving is sufficient to provide an adequate income in retirement. Given the likelihood that compulsion would be set at a moderate rate—for reasons of political acceptability—it could actually induce a false sense of complacency among employees—and employers.

The CBI therefore believes the Government should resist calls for compulsory contributions to private pension schemes as it is neither desirable nor necessary—and neither is there any evidence that it will provide the long-term solution we are searching for. Instead, given the right framework and incentives—the CBI believes that the voluntary approach can continue to deliver.

For the voluntary system to deliver for pensioners, a combination of reforms will be needed. The pressure on private provision is well documented—costs are rising as a result of rising life expectancy, falling investment returns as well as adverse taxation and regulatory changes. This has created large pension fund deficits—over £100bn—in defined benefit schemes requiring additional contributions of as much as £6bn a year.

While employers remain committed to occupational pensions, the nature of their involvement is likely to change in the future. Some will retain defined benefit, salary-related provision but others have chosen to move to defined contribution schemes. The costs and risks associated with pension provision will mean that the smallest companies, struggling to compete and grow their businesses, will choose to rely on the state second tier.

The CBI agrees with the analysis in the Pensions Commission's interim report that the UK faces some unpalatable choices. However, the CBI believes a combination of the three policy options can deliver a sustainable approach:

- saving more through occupational or stakeholder pensions;
- saving more through state provision—on a funded or pay as you go basis;
- increased participation in the labour market by more older workers.

Despite the critics of voluntarism, the CBI believes that a new and concerted effort to build on the existing voluntary approach has a real chance of increasing savings and pension provision in the UK. The focus for government should therefore be on making the climate for private pensions more attractive. The CBI believes that the voluntary system can be reinvigorated by:

- encouraging more employers to provide—and employees to take up—good quality pension provision;
- incentivising employers—and in particular SMEs—to provide pensions by maintaining existing tax reliefs and by further efforts to reduce and simplify the regulatory burden on occupational pensions (especially for hybrid schemes);
- ensuring individuals have sufficient financial information and education to better inform their retirement savings choices.

## Increase labour market participation among older workers

The third element to tackling the emerging pensions crisis is to encourage more people to extend their working lives. Employers are not expecting employees to work until they drop. However, with an ageing but healthier population, the CBI believes that it is inevitable that more people will want to work longer and that employers will want their skills. The UK has a good track record on participation rates of 50-64 year-olds in comparison to much of the rest of the EU. But there is no room for complacency—nearly 40 per cent of 55-64 year old men have dropped out of the labour market as well as over half of all women in the same age group. The Government's first priority should be to increase participation rates among this group of individuals—planned efforts to amend eligibility rules for incapacity benefit could help in this regard. Employers and government also need to work together to deliver improved emloyability for older workers who lack key skills.

The CBI believes that employers and employees should move away from the rigid approach to retirement that has prevailed in the past. Making older workers chose between the jobs they have always done or nothing leaves too many employees—and employers—with no choice at all. The loss of older workers' skills is unsustainable and we need to convince people that the state pension age should respond to changes in the labour market and life expectancy. Raising the state pension age would be an important signal to workers that they must be prepared to work longer (if they have not saved enough) and would reinforce other policies to encourage greater workforce participation among older workers. The CBI believes that the state pension age should be increased on a phased basis between 2020 and 2030. Such a move would help finance a more generous basic state pension. Raising the state pension age must be a policy for the medium term so that people have time to prepare and adjust.

However, a rise in the pension age to 70 would not cover the full cost of a rise in the basic state pension to the level of Guarantee Credit, and we therefore accept that the proportion of state spending dedicated to pensioners' incomes will need to rise over the long-term. This is, however, a long-term gradual shift, beyond the realm of current spending plans and projections, and should not imply an automatic increase in the burden of taxation. Over time, more resources can be devoted to pension provision without necessarily raising the burden of taxation by reallocating spending priorities, improving the efficiency of public spending and benefiting from economic growth.

# 6 | Brendan Barber  TUC

This pamphlet raises some of the key questions that we have spent the past few years debating—what to do about pensions? Much of the discussion over the last two years has suggested that the UK's pension system is in crisis. While it is undeniable that there are significant problems, it is important to distinguish between short, medium and long-term effects—and to be clear about who may be adversely affected, when and why.

Demographics are at the heart of the problem. The collapse of stock markets in recent years has inflicted major short-term pressures on pension funds, as did the decision of some firms to take pension holidays when times were good. But the underlying challenge is that life expectancy has been rising strongly and is going to go on increasing for the foreseeable future.

The debate on pensions reform has been crystallised by the Pensions Commission's interim report. Much of the debate now focuses on the four options outlined by the commission. We agree with the Commission that preserving the status quo, with the consequence that pensioners on average get poorer compared with the rest of society, is not acceptable. So other options for reform must be addressed. It is right to say that there is no easy option.

## State pensions and the state pension age

The key underlying assumption underpinning pensions policy that the share of provision would shift from the state to individuals is no longer realistic. Future pension policy will have to be based on the assumption that the state will have to sustain a bigger share of pension provision in the future than it does today.

The TUC, CBI and many others agree that the level of the basic state pension must increase. The problems arise when considering how to pay for any increase—for example, though higher taxation, increased state pension age, or cuts in other parts of the current state pension system.

Some further increase in tax/national insurance to pay for pensions in the future is certainly economically feasible. The UK currently ranks eighteenth out of 28 OECD economies in terms of the share of GDP for tax. However, as the recent election showed, there is no political consensus about whether this share is about right, too high, or too low. Employers have been vociferous in arguing that they should be exempt from making any further contribution through the tax system.

So increasing tax to pay for better pensions is always going to be controversial and difficult for any government to implement. And even if the political constraints could be overcome, it would not be economically realistic to expect the entire projected increase in the cost of pensions to be met through increased taxation.

Resources might also be found by spending less on other benefits. The Government has, for example, already significantly reduced spending on unemployment related benefits. The commitment to an 80 per cent employment rate may free up other resources in the long term by getting back into work many of the 2 million people of working age who are 'economically inactive' but who say they want a job.

One option for paying for a higher basic state pension is to increase the state pension age. The TUC is opposed to any increase in the State pension age or the ages in occupational pension schemes when an unreduced pension is payable. A key reason is that it is impossible to apply such a measure equitably. The most recent official figures for life expectancies show that on average life expectancies are much lower in Britain's poorer communities. This is in sharp contrast with much more equal societies such as Sweden where an explicit link between the state retirement age and life expectancy has recently been introduced.

One option yet to be actively explored in the UK debate would be to tie future long term increases in retirement age to increased longevity for the poorest in society, so future governments worried about spending more on pensions have an incentive to improve living standards for the worst off. But we would have to have clear evidence that the historic divides in longevity within British society were significantly closing before this could be considered as a realistic option.

However, there is far more that could be done to encourage voluntary working on beyond state retirement age and reduce early retirement. The Government has done much to address both issues, but actual implementation in the workplace is often patchy and falls far short of what is required. Work needs to be reorganised to make it more attractive to older workers and also more flexible, so the option of working part time is more widely available.

Much of the debate on pension reform has centred on addressing the problems of disincentives and complexity through the introduction of a Universal or Citizen's pension, typically offering a flat-rate benefit to all on the basis of residency. The TUC believes that the arguments about disincentives from the current system of pension credits are overstated, and that the credits have been extremely effective in getting help to the poorest pensioners. Some proponents of Universal Pension want to pay for it either by increasing the state retirement age or abolishing the second state pension—neither of which would command trade union support.

However, there are other significant advantages in moving away from means-testing to greater universal provision—not least in ensuring very high take-up and improved entitlement for low paid women workers. The TUC is actively looking at this option as one way forward in the pensions debate.

The TUC are strong supporters of second tier state pension. The TUC is committed to a revitalised state second pension system as part of an overall approach to introduce greater compulsion. The state second pension is the only practical vehicle for providing a second pension for workers on low pay; or with gaps in their employment for family responsibilities.

## Compulsion and incentives

Although some consensus is emerging on possible reforms to the State system, there is less consensus on reform to the private system. The debate on private pension reform has focused on the arguments between compulsion and incentives. Compulsion already exists in the UK. So the debate around compulsion is not about the principle, but how far compulsion should be increased.

The mood towards further compulsion has changed. Many now support the idea of compelling employees to join suitable schemes offered by their employers. However, the same organisations which advocate this form of compulsion for workers often illogically oppose compelling employers to make contributions.

Some employers, however, are persuaded that the creation of a level playing field would be beneficial. The Engineering Employers Federation 2004 pension survey found that two thirds of respondents supported compulsion on employers to make pension contributions, a major increase on the level of support two years earlier. Significantly, the surge in support came mainly from small and medium-sized employers.

One of the alternatives to compulsion often canvassed is enhanced fiscal incentives to encourage more individual saving and scheme redesign, drawing on the experience in the US. Unfortunately, neither history nor the international experiences are encouraging.

Household saving rates over the past forty years have gone up and down with the economic cycle but have otherwise been completely unresponsive to the fiscal incentives and endless exhortation to save introduced by successive governments. And coverage of pension schemes in the US is no higher than in the UK.

There are important questions to be addressed on how a system of compulsion might work in practice and our interim submission to the Pensions Commission sets out some options and issues. One is risk. If the government is compelling people to save, it must also lay down stringent standards for the governance and design features of the schemes they are being asked to save into.

Another is the savings vehicle. In reality, most people will be saving into some form of money purchase schemes. Many are good schemes, but we would like to see more attention given to the encouragement of hybrid schemes and to industry wide schemes, drawing on the successful scheme operated for many years in the building and civil engineering sector. Both could help reduce risk, improve security for savers, and reduce costs for employers.

A third is making provision for the low paid, where a revitalised second state pension may offer a more secure and better alternative than private provision. A key problem with the latter is that in order to turn a profit, private providers levy high charges or commissions, so that modest savers end up with very poor returns.

## Consensus and institutional safeguards

Pension policy over the past twenty-five years has been characterised by frequent government interventions and policy changes, often with little public debate about their long-term consequences and no regard for the need to sustain a political or industrial consensus. It is no surprise that politicians and governments are not trusted by people when it comes to their future pensions. Meanwhile, the many past shortcomings of the financial service industry mean there is little trust in the market either.

The Pensions Commission has already performed a great service in providing a clear, authoritative and above all independent analysis of the challenges and options for reform. But once the Commission issues its final report later this year, it will disband.

Successful pensions policy is about long-term reform and long-term reform works best with a degree of political and industrial consensus. But while we should make every effort to build such a consensus, it cannot be an excuse to forever put off necessary reforms.

But even more importantly, we need a permanent institutional safeguard against arbitrary political intervention by a future government and against the shortcomings of the market. A permanent body independent of government would help restore confidence by providing early warnings of new challenges, making recommendations for action, and ensuring that agreed reforms are kept on track.

# 7 | Ian Naismith  Scottish Widows

Scottish Widows welcomes this pamphlet by John Denham and Richard Brooks as a valuable contribution to the current policy debate on pensions reform. It lays out clearly the main issues to be addressed and, crucially, the necessary components for achieving a robust consensus for the future.

Whatever reforms are eventually put in place to state provision, everyone agrees that we need a significant increase to private pension provision through the savings of individuals and their employers. The pensions industry has a key role to play in developing appropriate, good value products, in distributing them effectively and in helping to educate the general public on the need to save for retirement. However, to maximise provision for retirement there must be an appropriate legislative framework in place, and in this brief response we consider what it should be.

## State pensions, incentives and disincentives to save
The legislative framework can act as an incentive to save or as a disincentive. The main incentive is, of course, financial. Under the current UK system this incentive for individuals comes through tax relief on money paid into pensions, some tax benefits during the period when funds are invested, and a tax-free lump sum at retirement. For employers, the incentive is a reduction to the level of Corporation Tax.

The fact that employer contributions are not subject to National Insurance contributions gives some incentive to provide remuneration as pension contributions rather than as increased salary. Taken together, these tax benefits should represent a considerable incentive to save in a pension. However, they are not currently well presented and therefore not well understood.

There are two key disincentives. One is financial, because the tax and benefits system disadvantages some savers, and the other is the sheer complexity of the UK pensions system. Even the currently proposed 'simplification' is enormously complex, although ultimately it should genuinely make pensions easier for all but the very wealthy—most of us will be able to pay as much as we want to into our pensions whenever we can afford to. However, a major problem with the UK pensions system at present is that the two key disincentives (financial loss and complexity) both feature in the foundational pension to which most people are entitled—the Basic State Pension.

The level of Basic State Pension is deliberately set below the official poverty line and some way below an income that would be considered acceptable even for the very poorest. This is designed to make the system affordable to the Government by capping the state benefit paid to those with significant private income.

The Government aims to ensure that everyone has an acceptable living standard by topping up Basic State Pension, where necessary, to the 'Guarantee Credit' level. For a single person entitled to full Basic State Pension but with no other income or significant assets, the top-up is currently £27.40 a week. However, if that individual has a modest amount of other income, the top-up is reduced under the pension credit by 40p for every £1 of personal income. Since any pension contributions made by that individual would almost certainly only attract 22 per cent tax relief, there is a real financial loss compared with spending the income when it was first received. The tax-free lump sum from a pension plan only partially compensates for that loss.

As well as the financial disincentive, the current system also has an evident complexity, which is increased by the means-testing required to establish eligibility for the Pension Credit. There is also further complexity in the State Second Pension.

The current system may be viewed as a delicate compromise that satisfies many government objectives, including long-term affordability and targeting towards the poorest in society. But for many people the disincentives to save outweigh these benefits, and there is general agreement that reform is needed.

As Denham and Brooks point out, there is widespread support for increasing the Basic State Pension to broadly the level of the current Guarantee Credit. Scottish Widows believes this is highly desirable. While receipt of a higher state pension means that people will need less private income than at present to achieve a comparable living standard, the inherent simplicity of such a system, and the removal of the financial disincentive to save, should mean that savings increase rather than decrease.

Such a change would, of course, have to be paid for. That would almost certainly involve radical reform of the State Second Pension, and probably its phasing out. While that would mean reduced state pensions for some, it would further simplify the system and would mean that those who are self-employed or who have to spend long periods out of the labour market would not be disadvantaged as they are at present. I will consider the impact on contracting-out later.

Increasing the Basic State Pension would probably also involve a phased increase to the state pension age. We recognise the particular issues this could create for manual workers. But it seems intrinsically sensible that when we are all living longer, and often starting our careers later than in the past, the age at which we retire should be based on working for a fairly constant percentage of our average lifespan. The situation of manual workers could be addressed by allowing state pensions to start after a set period of National Insurance contributions (perhaps 45 years), regardless of age.

## Contracting out and the rebates

There then remains the question of contracting-out. At current rebate levels, contracting-out is much less attractive to consumers than when it was first introduced. However, it still has benefits over the State Second Pension, including the flexibility it offers, for example to start receiving a pension earlier and (from April 2006) to take part of the benefits as a tax-free lump sum. For a group of consumers this flexibility justifies the significant risk of losing out financially compared with being contracted-in. There are also many people who simply do not trust any government to deliver on its pension promises and prefer to have their own fund building up.

A less tangible benefit of contracting-out is the incentive it gives to save more on top of the rebates and its effect in keeping down policy charges. The successful introduction of personal pensions in 1988 was built on a combination of high levels of contracting-out and significant supplementary personal contributions. This effect has been lost in recent years because the number of people contracting out for the first time has plummeted, and contracting-out now tends to be something considered after a decision has been made to pay into a pension. If rebates were to be set at a more attractive level, contracting-out could again help boost saving by individuals, although the impact of that should not be overstated—it is a much smaller incentive than, say, employer contributions into a pension.

The impact of contracting-out rebates on pension policy charges is difficult to quantify, but there is a beneficial effect. The rebates not only help providers like Scottish Widows provide economies of scale but also benefit from lower administrative costs because they are paid automatically by the government rather than having to be collected by the provider. For many providers, the ability to play in the 'one per cent world' of stakeholder pensions was partly driven by the prospect of contracting-out rebates.

Clearly, if the State Second Pension were to be phased out, contracting-out as we currently know it would also be discontinued.

However, it would still be possible to have a form of contracting-out which could apply to, say, the tier of the Basic State Pension between its current level and our proposed higher level.

Looking beyond state pensions, the key to adequate pension savings for a majority of the population and the most effective form of distribution from a provider perspective is the active involvement of employers. The desire to get 'something for nothing' means that many people are happy to pay into a pension scheme to which their employer also contributes, even where they would not otherwise save of their own volition.

This suggests that focusing on encouraging employers to establish and pay into pension arrangements could disproportionately improve overall pension provision. This could be through carrots—for example, a National Insurance reduction for employers making significant pension contributions—or through sticks—for example, by forcing employers to match voluntary employee contributions. In considering the role of employers, the second report of the Pensions Commission will build on the work of both the Employer Taskforce and the stream relating to the workplace in the Financial Services Authority's Financial Capability initiative.

## The way forward

We support a continuing role for the Pensions Commission as an independent analytical resource, and would like to see direct representation from pension providers. While such a body could only have limited powers in dealing with matters that have financial consequences for Government, it could have much more authority in proposing measures to simplify administration.

Scottish Widows believes that a political consensus is essential if we are to make real progress in improving saving for retirement. Very quick action should be taken on matters where that consensus already exists—for example, auto-enrolment of employees into good quality pensions unless they actively opt out. Beyond that, we need an informed debate following the second report of the Pensions Commission later this year, and we support Denham and Brooks' suggestion of bringing key stakeholders together in an attempt to achieve consensus.

# 8 | Alison O'Connell and Chris Curry  PPI

The new Labour Government's manifesto commitment to long-term reform, seeking consensus in a National Debate, puts the politics of pension reform centre-stage. The Fabian Society is to be congratulated for leading the debate on how to get the politics right.

The Pensions Policy Institute (PPI), an independent expert research organisation, recognised early that reform of state pensions is needed. We undertook a programme of research on state pension reform, and have been keeping an inventory of the many proposals to come onto the table.

Like all good pamphlets, this one prompts many ideas for how to take the debate forward. Our reflections cover the ways in which we would hope the political debate continues from now: to develop pension reform proposals, to make them happen and then keep policy stable.

We have three suggestions for policy makers as they grapple with the pension reform challenges:

- Commit to evidence-based trade-offs;
- Build consensus on objectives first, method later;
- Think creatively about maintaining the consensus.

## Commit to evidence-based trade-offs

Pension policy is a tricky subject. Even technical experts tend to be knowledgeable about only part of it. There is a lot of detail, some of it critical for policy decision making. We have known influential people on the pensions scene who were unaware that not everyone gets a full Basic State Pension in their own right. For the record, 35 per cent of all people over state pension age do not, and women are still expected to have a Basic State Pension on average 15 per cent lower than men in 2021.[10]

To achieve pension reform good enough to last for the long-term, it is self-evident that it should be developed with the correct interpretation of the right facts. However, pension myths can develop because they are easy to grasp. They then take root as they are politically more useful than the reality, making any later attempt at reform more difficult.

For example, the reason often given for ruling out raising the state pension age is the inequality in life expectancies between regions or social classes. This inequality exists, although it is often exaggerated by referring to historical data and by measuring life expectancy at birth rather than at the more relevant current state pension age.[11]

The more important fact not given such airtime is that longevity is improving for everyone, to which raising state pension age is a logical response. Expected length of life after age 65 for men in the professional group has increased by 25 per cent since the mid 1970s, whilst that for unskilled manual workers has increased by over 15 per cent.[12] Even the smaller improvement significantly increases the cost of pensions.

By itself, the inequality in life expectancy should not rule out raising state pension age, provided that policy reflects the fact that life expectancy has improved more slowly for poorer people than affluent people, and action continues to reduce health inequalities wherever possible.

Because the inequality argument was used in relation to state pension age, the same argument was able to be made against government proposals to increase the normal pension age in public sector pensions.

The logic of raising the state pension age to deal with improving longevity is not going to go away, and if any government ever does want to make the case for doing so, it will face a harder battle because of its own arguments against.

This is not to leap to the conclusion that raising state pension age is the right policy, but rather that such a policy choice should be made on the basis of the correct facts. As Brooks and Denham say, these pensions policy trade-offs now have to be confronted, and gaining broad public consent will be challenging. Pensions now cost more than they used to, largely because we are all living longer, so we will have to spend more money to keep them at constant value, let alone improve them. This means that politicians will not be able to reform without having to break bad news.

We are only beginning the debate on where that bad news might fall. A logical starting point is to understand what the role of the state realistically can be, given the resources we are prepared to put into pensions:

- Should the state try to prevent or ameliorate poverty in old age, or go further?
- What share of GDP should the state spend on pension benefits and on incentivising private saving?
- Should this share increase as the number of older people increases, or stay the same?

Most organisations involved in pensions say that the state first tier should be improved. This will cost more than the current system. A good second tier as well will need a further commitment to tax rises, as well as an increase in state pension age, or a cutback in the amount of tax relief given to private pension saving. Yet all these have been 'no-go' areas in political debate so far.

Proposals are being made without looking at the cost, although it is very unlikely that they could be afforded. The electorate is not being sensitised to these issues, but if we do not face up to them, we may end up with a generous new pension that cannot be afforded after the first five years.

Brooks and Denham's question on the trade-off between improving the first tier as far as possible or having a second tier is therefore critical. The facts needed to have an evidence-based debate about this issue are not appreciated by most pension influencers, let alone the public. It is not easy to do the economic modelling necessary to understand the implications of such questions as:

- How much more would the policy options cost?
- Which would be better for particular groups: women, carers, lower earners?
- What is best for older pensioners?

## Build consensus on objectives first, method later

As Brooks and Denham say, it will be impossible to please everyone, and consensus should not be interpreted as that. The pamphlet also refers to PPI analysis of the reform proposals being made by various organisations. It is clear from these proposals that there is consensus for a simple basic tier of state pension that takes as many people as possible above the means-testing level. Different methods are proposed to do this.

This is because policy is usually developed from a report or consultation document written by very few people. Written submissions are made, and some 'oral evidence' taken from a few organisations. The original report writers come back with a refined proposal, which is taken up by government for a Green Paper and White Paper which follows the same pattern.

Organisations have tended to respond to this process by developing their own proposals for pension reform inevitably taking into account what would be best for the interests that their organisation represents. These proposals are usually defined by 'products', for example, introduce a Citizen's Pension, scrap or keep contracting-out, change tax relief to matching contributions. Because the proposals look different, there are headlines in the media saying that organisations disagree. Actually, they are often proposing different ways of getting to very similar objectives. The risk is that organisations are boxed into a corner of supporting only one method.

Instead of keeping experts and practitioners out of the process until asking for responses in a structured consultation process, a better approach might involve them directly in the development of the proposals. By involving experts early, consensus can be sought around objectives first, and then methods developed to meet the shared goals. The experts can talk and listen to each other, not just talk to government.

PPI seminars tend to attract a diverse group of attendees. We get positive feedback on how useful it is for pensions people to meet each other and hear first hand other views and experiences. This is rare: most pension managers spend time with other pension fund managers, academics with academics and so on.

So the PPI is very supportive of the new Government's National Debate on pensions, provided that it brings together early experts and influencers from across the pensions community who have committed to considering the necessary trade-offs with evidence and open minds.


## Think creatively about maintaining the consensus

A woman aged 40 now has around a one in four chance of living beyond 95. She would surely wish for a stable pensions policy to last over that lifetime of 11 or more parliamentary terms. So, having developed a pensions policy reform with, we hope, a fair degree of political and expert consensus, how can we maintain stability? Long-term stability is not guaranteed by a political consensus, but it must help. It would be more difficult for any politician to make a negative change if that involved being obviously different from the agreed starting point.

Mechanisms to make departures from the starting point obvious should, therefore, be helpful.

One mechanism is to make the policy as simple as possible, so that any changes to it cannot be done without everyone noticing. Having one state pension, defined as a percentage of National Average Earnings, payable from state pension age, has just two parameters; three if you differentiate the amount for individuals in a couple; four including a residency criterion. The current system, conservatively, has around 100 parameters.

Another idea is an 'Accord' on the framework for the state pension system signed by political parties. As used in New Zealand, the Accord includes general principles for a pension system, as well as the minimum and maximum level of the state pension as a percentage of National Average Earnings. If the government of the day contemplates any change to the state pension, it has to consult formally with any party who signed the Accord first. Any change to the key parameters would therefore be highly transparent. A mechanism like New Zealand's Accord could be a way of reducing the risk of sudden, hidden policy change on the basic state pension structure while still enabling political debate on wider pensions policy, such as private pensions.

Another mechanism mentioned in the Fabian Society pamphlet is the independent body of experts. Experts are unelected, and elected politicians should make the decisions. So, we should think carefully about having an independent body making any decisions about pensions policy. A body of experts could make recommendations based on pre-agreed criteria (such as 'What should state pension age in 2030 be so that the average length of time a pension is received for the cohort then at state pension age is the same as it is for the cohort aged 65 today, taking into account ... etc?') but the decision to change state pension age would have to be subject to parliamentary scrutiny.

The reforms now being discussed really could be the once in a generation opportunity for positive change in pensions policy. The pensions community is not resisting change—in fact it is increasingly vocal in calling for reform. The challenge now is to tackle some of the politically difficult realities. We believe that to do so successfully, politicians should commit to making evidence-based policy-making, should build on the consensus that exists on the fundamental objectives for reform, and should seek ways to maintain the consensus.

# 9 | Christine Farnish  NAPF

The National Association of Pension Funds was established in 1923 to lobby for an enabling fiscal regime to encourage the growth of funded pensions. The successful growth of such schemes during the last century is testimony in part to our success. Eighty years on, the NAPF still represents the interests of occupational pension schemes, with nearly 90 per cent of funded UK schemes in our membership by size of scheme. But our purpose has become broader, and our mission today is 'to encourage and promote fair and decent retirement provision, especially through the workplace'.

We, like other commentators, have expressed concern about the weakness in the UK's overall pensions system in recent years. In 2002 we published a paper 'Pensions—Plain and Simple' which recommended reform of the state pension system and a simpler regulatory and incentives framework for the funded sector.

Since then we have done considerably more work on the pensions reform agenda, and have concluded that the most pressing requirement is to reshape and simplify what the state provides to pensioners. It may seem odd that the organisation representing workplace pension saving should start here; but we see it as the absolute priority. Unless and until we reform the state system, we will not be able to reinvigorate and sustain a healthy funded sector on top.

Our view is that the money currently spent on the basic state pensions, S2P and pension credit would be more effective if repackaged into a simple first-tier pension, indexed with average earnings and available to all at state pension age. We have called this a 'Citizen's Pension', and have suggested it be a universal pension based on a residency test, to avoid the need for complex arrangements to credit-in savers, people with broken work records and the like. Our modelling work shows that a Citizen's Pension set at £109 per person per week could be affordable now with no additional resources needed, but would probably cost more than the current system (depending on assumptions about future saving rates and pension credit uptake) by around 2030, unless adjustments were made to state pension age. Such adjustments will almost certainly be needed anyway before 2050, based on current longevity data.

A Citizen's Pension could still be 'paid for' by National Insurance contributions paid by those of working age and able to work. As Beveridge originally envisaged, it would be a contributory state pension, paid at a flat rate and universally available. It would thus be on a par with the National Health Service; ostensibly 'paid for' through National Insurance contributions but a universal service available to all at point of need. Hopefully such a simple system would have something else in common with the National Health Service: the benefit, and the entitlement to it, would become so well understood, and be so strongly supported, that any attempt by politicians to fiddle with it would be resisted by voters. This would help protect it from future political risk.

The main benefit of a Citizen's Pension lies in its simplicity. A very clear message could be given to consumers: you will get £109 a week, no more and no less, when you reach state pension age. This would incentivise saving, or longer working, or more likely both—especially if the system was designed to give a higher Citizen's Pension to people at a slightly later age. A modest degree of means testing might still be needed but it would be for the few not the many, thus not distorting incentives to save.

Provision by the state of basic security for all, which allowed people to live in decency in their old age, would allow significant deregulation

## Contracting out—trends

|  | 94/95 | 99/00 | 02/03 |
|---|---|---|---|
| Total employees m | 22.9 | 25.1 | 25.8 |
| Contracted in all | 6.4 | 8.7 | 13.6* |
| Contracted out (public DB) | 4.0 | 4.5 | 5.0 |
| Contracted out (private DB) | 4.0 | 3.6 | 3.2 |
| Contracted out (occupational DC) | 0.6 | 0.7 | 0.6 |
| Contracted out (personal pensions) | 4.1 | 3.8 | 3.5 |

Source: DWP Second Tier Pension Provision

*includes 4m people credited in to S2P

of the funded system (both occupational schemes and personal pensions), thus removing many of the current disincentives faced by employers and product providers in making pensions widely available. Employers would then be able to put in place benefits packages, including ways of helping employees save for their retirement, that met their particular business needs. The current tax regime for pension saving could be reformed and replaced with more effective incentives targeted at employers (even the self-employed have employers: themselves!) to encourage uptake of retirement saving schemes.

One feature of NAPF's proposals that has proved controversial to some has been the removal of National Insurance contracting-out rebates, which have been a feature of the current system since the 1970's. It is true that we would prefer a single tier of state provision, and that in order to maintain the cost to the public purse at its current level we would scrap S2P, rebates and pension credit to deliver a universal pension at guarantee credit levels. Some claim that this would damage the existing UK private pension system and reduce the prospect of more retirement saving in the future. We do not share that view. Stopping contracting out does not mean less pension for anyone. It simply means that one part of the overall pension moves from being provided by a scheme or pension provider to it being provided by the state.

The fact is that NI rebates, while a useful incentive in the early years of occupational schemes some 30 years ago, are no longer a significant element in the overall funded system.

It can be seen from the table (above) that there is a steady and growing trend for employees to contract back into the second state pension. Contracting out is only on the increase in public sector DB schemes, probably because of increased membership of those schemes. Most of these are, of course, unfunded, so removal of rebates would not 'take money from the funded system'. Most occupational DC schemes were set up on a contracted-in basis; and virtually no new contracted-out personal pension business is being sold, because of future misselling risk (persuading people to contract out into a personal pension is asking them to forgo a certain, government backed DB benefit for an uncertain, market risk-related DC benefit). Indeed, some larger personal pension providers are automatically contracting back in their existing pension customers, because they are so concerned about this risk down the track.

That leaves private sector occupation DB schemes. About £3-4bn of the overall £11bn p.a. rebate money ends up in these schemes which are largely traditional final salary schemes, now closed to new member and struggling with deficits. The rebate money represents around 15 per cent of the money going into them.

Most private sector sponsoring employers would welcome the opportunity to reduce the level of cost and risk in these legacy schemes by handing back a relatively modest part of the overall benefit promised—together with the rebate money—to the state. The schemes involved would end up carrying less cost and risk to the sponsor and thus the cost of keeping them going (or at least, funding them to provide the current accrued level of promised benefits) would be less of a burden. The overall benefit level in these schemes would be redesigned so as to offset the value of a more generous state pension against a lower pension scheme benefit. Getting rid of contracting out would also reduce a lot of the administrative cost and complexity involved in running such schemes.

Some argue that such an opportunity for scheme redesign could lead to the closure of more DB schemes. It is true that any requirement to make major changes to schemes might prompt such a decision. However, the fact is that around three quarters of all private sector DB schemes are already closed to new entrants and many of these are already considering or embarked upon a process of closure to future accruals, in the light of cost pressures and the need to cap the level of risk to the company from the pension scheme. An external prompt to changes in scheme design is already in the pipeline—in the form of the new pensions tax regime from April 2006. The removal of rebates and S2P equivalent liabilities for schemes should be neutral in its overall effect. It is just as plausible to argue that DB schemes would be more likely to stay open if they could reduce their liabilities in this way, and such a change to the overall system could reinvigorate DB or other risk forms of scheme design.

To conclude, we firmly believe that if the funded pensions sector is to grow and flourish in future, a simpler state system with a more generous safety net benefit for all is required.

# References

1. Emmerson C and Disney R (2005), *Public pension reform in the United Kingdom: what effect on the financial well being of current and future pensioners?*

2. DWP long-term projections available at http://www.dwp.gov.uk/asd/asd4/LT3.xls. Benefits include the Basic State Pension, S2P, Pension Credit, Winter Fuel Payments, over-75s TV Licences and Christmas Bonus. Figures exclude contracted out rebates and the value of tax relief on pension saving.

3. DWP *ibid.*

4. Government Actuary's Department Quinquennial Review Update available at http://www.gad.gov.uk/publications/social_insurance.htm.

5. Inland Revenue estimates available at http://www.hmrc.gov.uk/stats/pensions/menu.htm. Excludes National Insurance relief on employer contributions.

6. PPI / Age Concern 'Tax relief and incentives for pension saving' http://www.pensionspolicyinstitute.org.uk/news.asp?s=2.

7. PPI 'Should state pensions be contributory or universal?' forthcoming.

8. Pensions Commission first report fig.1.11.

9. Richard Greenhalgh was until July 2004 Chairman of Unilever UK.

10. PQ Frank Field MP, Hansard 13 December 2004: Column 861W; Curry & O'Connell (2003) *The Pensions Landscape*, Pensions Policy Institute.

11. See PPI Briefing Note 17, 'How big is the life expectancy gap by social class?' for a fuller explanation.

12. PPI analysis from ONS statistics.